DEAR HEARTBREAK

DEAR HEARTBREAK

YA AUTHORS AND TEENS ON THE DARK SIDE OF LOVE

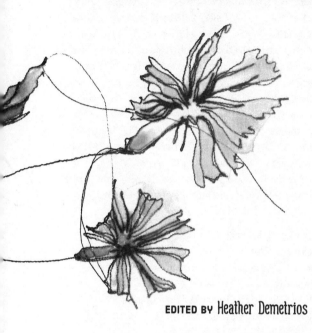

EDITED BY Heather Demetrios

LETTERS FROM REAL TEENS ANSWERED WITH CARE BY

Becky Albertalli * Adi Alsaid * Libba Bray * Mike Curato
Heather Demetrios * Amy Ewing * Zach Fehst * Gayle Forman
Corey Ann Haydu * Varian Johnson * A.S. King * Nina LaCour
Kim Liggett * Kekla Magoon * Sarah McCarry * Sandhya Menon
Cristina Moracho * Jasmine Warga * Ibi Zboi

HENRY HOLT AND COMPANY
NEW YORK

Henry Holt and Company, *Publishers since 1866*
Henry Holt® is a registered trademark of Macmillan Publishing Group, LLC
175 Fifth Avenue, New York, NY 10010 • fiercereads.com

Library of Congress Cataloging-in-Publication Data
Names: Demetrios, Heather, editor.
Title: Dear heartbreak : YA authors and teens on the dark side of love /
    edited by Heather Demetrios.
Description: First edition. | New York : Henry Holt and Company, 2018. |
    Includes bibliographical references and index.
Identifiers: LCCN 2018003710 | ISBN 9781250170903
Subjects: LCSH: Love. | Rejection (Psychology) | Emotions.
Classification: LCC BF575.L8 D386 2018 | DDC 155.5/192—dc23
LC record available at https://lccn.loc.gov/2018003710

Our books may be purchased in bulk for promotional, educational, or business use. Please contact your local bookseller or the Macmillan Corporate and Premium Sales Department at (800) 221-7945 ext. 5442 or by e-mail at MacmillanSpecialMarkets@macmillan.com.

First edition, 2018 / Designed by Liz Dresner
Printed in the United States of America
10 9 8 7 6 5 4 3 2 1

For the heartbroken

WE DARE YOU TO READ THIS BOOK ABOUT HOW SHITTY LOVE CAN BE

(AN INTRODUCTION)

Love is a beast.

There are plenty of books about how love is rainbows and roses and butterfly kisses, but this is not one of them.

Sorry.

This is a book about the dark side of love: the way it kicks your ass, tears out your heart, and then forces you to eat it, bite by bloody bite. If you've felt this way, you are not alone. And if you haven't felt this way, we promise you will. Not to be a downer, but it kind of comes with the territory of being human. This is also a book about how you can survive love. How you can be broken and battered by a relationship (or lack of one) and still have the real deal, when the real deal is good and ready to show up. Better yet, it's about how you don't even need someone to show up because the kind of love that will save you every time is the love you give yourself. I'm not feeding you a sappy self-help platitude here. This is not a Hallmark card or an inspirational mug you can buy at the bookstore (although mugs, bookstores, and snail mail are all wonderful). Loving yourself is damn hard because it means accepting all the parts of you that you can't stand. It means knowing you're actually okay even though society wants you to believe that you aren't. It's downright revolutionary.

Oscar Wilde said that "the heart was made to be broken." I don't know if that's true, but I know that after hearts break, they can be put back together in new and startling ways, and you're forever different because of it. Our hearts are resilient. They can go a hundred rounds in the ring, get knocked out, and the next day be right back in there, fists up. But how do you keep from getting the shit beaten out of you by love? What do you do when you're against the ropes?

When you're in love or out of love or can't freaking *find* love, it can be hard to know which way is up. What are you supposed to say to someone who's stomped all over your heart? How can you possibly go on living and eating and brushing your hair when you lose someone you love, or when the person you love barely knows you exist? Love messes with your head. It can sometimes make you feel like you don't deserve it, and it definitely makes you feel like it's the most important thing in the world. (Actually, it is. Love is what it's all about.) The Beatles weren't lying when they said, "All you need is love." If we, as humans, need love as much as we need oxygen, then how the hell are we supposed to stay alive when it takes a hike or doesn't show up at all? No one tells you what to do when it turns into some creepy alien shit intent on sucking out your life force. No one explains that it can be agonizing, an exquisitely wretched pain we'd give almost anything to never, ever feel again.

That's where this book comes in. I asked young adults all over the world to write a letter to Heartbreak—they could say or ask whatever they wanted, as long as they kept it real. Of those letters, the authors featured in this anthology each chose one to answer. They picked the letter that spoke to their heart, the letter they *had* to respond to. Each author in these pages has suffered from a broken heart. Some are married; some are single. Some are gay; some are straight. Some have been dumped, and some have been the dumper. Some have cheated; some have been betrayed. None of us are perfect. And the advice we give in these pages is not because we're licensed psychologists (although one of us is) or because we have it all figured out. We're being so bold as to give you our two cents because we spend a lot of time thinking about love and we've learned a couple of things along the way. When you write a story—any story—you're trying to figure out what it means to be human. And a big part of being human is falling in and out of love. Storyteller meet Reader. Reader, meet Storyteller.

Sylvia Plath said, "Perhaps some day I'll crawl back home, beaten, defeated. But not as long as I can make stories out of my heartbreak, beauty out of sorrow." These authors all talk about love in their books in one way or another. Sometimes it's epic and star-crossed, or it's confusion about whether they love a boy or girl—or both. Sometimes it's about being invisible and seemingly unloved, or feeling like they don't deserve love. Sometimes it's about falling in love with your best friend, or someone you've just met, or a boy who hurts you but that you can't seem to shake. They're able to write about love so well because they have all loved and lost and yearned and hoped. They've all wondered if "the One" is really out there, or if the idea of a soul mate is a total myth. Many have doubted their own worthiness, wondering what was so wrong with them that they couldn't even get a date. Their bravery in telling their own stories—and the courage of the people who wrote letters to Heartbreak—shows that no matter how awful love might seem, it's worth the cost of the ride.

The world is batshit crazy right now: racism, homophobia, intolerance, sexism, terrorism, and fear seem to be in charge. But they're not. Any good thing, any good person, is good because of love. Any time we see society change for the better, it's because a few brave souls chose love over hate. To love people in the volatile times we live in—romantically or otherwise—is an act of courage and defiance. We see this in how many people get married, even though the divorce rate is sky-high. Or in the boy who doesn't stop asking out the girl he's crushing on, even though she rejects him every damn time. We see it in the guy who forgives his boyfriend for cheating on him, but leaves anyway, because he loves *himself*, and knows he deserves better. (I'm going to let you in on a little secret: Loving yourself is a Jedi-knight level of love.) Love can be a political act, a radical life choice, a refusal to submit to a world that tries to put a price tag on everything that matters. Opening up your heart to someone and letting them in will be the scariest thing you'll ever do—and the best thing. Heartbreak is a natural part of this process. When your heart breaks, it creates fertile soil for the next love. Maybe it's a bit more tender; maybe it needs to be watered with a deluge of tears. I offer you these lyrics from U2's "Beautiful Day": "the heart is a bloom / shoots up from the stony ground." It can grow in the most unexpected places.

A note on the letters you're about to read:

In 2017, I visited some schools here in the US and, as I mentioned earlier in this ~~rant~~ introduction, put out a call online for teens to submit letters to Heartbreak about their bad times in the romance department. There was no guarantee that their letter would be chosen by one of the YA writers participating in this project, of course, but I'm a firm believer in the power of the letter never sent, so it didn't really matter if their letter ended up in the book or not: The writing was going to work some magic on their hearts anyway. I received letters from people all over the world. The teens who wrote in left it all on the stage—or, in our case, the page. They poured out their hearts, outed their haters, and confessed their deepest, darkest secrets and fears. I very lightly edited the letters for grammar and readability (my heart goes out to high school English teachers everywhere), and I omitted any details that could be identifying. More than anything, it was important to me that this was a book that holds space for the teens and YA writers brave enough to participate. In order to protect them, I've kept the teens' letters completely anonymous. We have letters here that come from various regions in the United States, Europe, and Mexico. (See? It doesn't matter where you're from—heartbreak will find you. No one is exempt. *cue ominous music*)

Shit gets real in these pages, and so I hope that after you read these letters, you'll send out your version of good vibes to the writers and to anyone (including yourself) who might be hurting in the ways our writers talk about. We got a lot of letters, and I wish I could publish them all. My big takeaway is this: Every single person you know is hurting. *Every single person.* There were letters about abuse at home, cheating, betrayal, rape, suicidal thoughts, suicide attempts, bone-crushing loneliness, LGBTQ+ haters, regret, unrequited love, and fear of deportation. There were poems and promises and letters that weren't for Heartbreak at all but to the parents and boyfriends and girlfriends who had broken the writer's heart. More than a few writers told Heartbreak to go fuck itself, which made me happy—I like that there are a bunch of mutinous people out there who refuse to go down without a fight. We need more people like that on the front lines of love.

And, holy hell, are you in for it when you read the responses to these letters from the young adult authors brave enough to say yes when I asked them to bleed all over the page. I am so honored to bear witness to their stories, and I know you will be, too. The authors featured here dug deep, excavating some of their most painful memories in order to help not just the teens who wrote in, but every single person reading these pages.

Their levels of vulnerability, raw candor, unexpected humor, and gut-wrenching storytelling make me proud to be human and grateful to be part of the writing tribe. I hope they inspire you to own *your* stories and to tell them, to have the courage to face the hard truths when they emerge, and to embrace hope and the possibility of awesome. I know for some of you it's really shit times and it might feel like you're in a dark hole you'll never see your way out of—I hope this book provides a map of sorts, or at least a little light that wasn't there before. Make sure to check out the back of the book for resources to get help if you need it.

So here's to the romantics, the cynics, the heartbroken, the hopeful. Here's to everyone who's ever been in love or will be in love. Here's to moonlight kisses and break-up playlists and shouting matches in parking lots. Here's to forgiveness and choosing yourself and saying *yes* when it scares the shit out of you—and screaming NO at the top of your lungs when you need to.

I hope these pages give you as much faith in love and in our ability to heal and learn and grow after we're hurt as they've given me. As a character in one of my favorite movies, *Love, Actually,* says, "Let's go get the shit kicked out of us by love."

Courage, dear heart.

Heather Demetrios

Brooklyn, 2018

This is a good sign, having a broken heart. It means we have tried for something.

—Elizabeth Gilbert

THE LETTERS

I don't think I'm unlovable. But I keep wondering:
what is my glitch?

—*The Upside of Unrequited*, Becky Albertalli

Dear Heartbreak,

Ever since I was a little girl I dreamed about true love—sounds ridiculous, right? Well, the thing is, I was always inspired about it because of movies and books my dad used to read to me. So one day I saw him. He was everything I dreamed of (or so I thought). His caramel eyes were full of mischief, like he was calling out for trouble, and don't even mention the hair and the smile—a total dream boat! I was so in love that I thought he was in love with me, but how could he be when he barely knew me?

I thought that because he did things like telling me I was special, different from all of the other girls—flirting with me (he pulled my hair to annoy me and he always used an excuse to touch me)—I created an illusion around him (big mistake). So one day I decided to confess my feelings. I was so full of confidence that he liked me back, but when I got to him, he was with another girl and I felt a flinch of jealousy. But I brushed it off. I was determined to confess my feelings—until I saw something that completely shattered my heart. He was kissing her and smiling at her and he had this twinkle in his eye and he was touching her gently, like touching her too hard might make her fall apart. I didn't know where to run or hide. I felt completely heartbroken.

The thing is, he still found out that I liked him: A dear friend of mine shattered my trust and told him because she also liked him! Great friend, huh? So the next day I went to school heart-broken about seeing him (I forgot to mention we went to the same school), and there I go to talk to him like always, but some-thing was very different. He looked at me like I was a bag of poop and ignored me. I was so confused and hurt. So the bell rings and we all go to the classroom (we also have the same class) and I was talking to a friend, but I was trying to catch the eye of the boy that I liked. When I finally got it, I waved at him and he looked me up and down in disgust and came to me. I gulped. I knew he knew, but the words that followed still hurt like a bitch: "You disgust me. Listen to me, I would never like someone like you—you are ugly and I hate you. I don't want you near me ever again, do you understand?"

God, those words almost made me cry (key word: almost). I gave him my best smile, even though I didn't mean it, and told him: "I understand; I hope you have a nice day and life." Then I went to my seat. When I glanced at him, he looked so confused. I hated myself because of him. To this day, I still think that no one will ever love me. All my dreams were shattered—and you know what's the worst part of it all? He still hates me and I don't even know why! I wish I'd never see him again, but the thing is, as time goes by I still don't hate him. He broke me, but I still don't hate him.

Love,

Unrequited Love, 16

YOU ARE SO FAR FROM BROKEN

Dear Unrequited Love,

I'll hate him for you.

I mean, wow. This guy's an actual shitstain. But you? You're beautiful. And you're brave. Look at what you did: You loved someone fearlessly. You got your heart broken. You went to school the next day anyway and got your heart broken again. You responded by showing him exactly what grace looks like. And here you are, picking yourself up and dusting yourself off every single day.

I was a lot like you when I was younger. I went to school. I had friends. But I had this entire inner romantic landscape, shaped by books and movies and fairy tales and hormones. I don't think I'll ever find the words to explain the sheer force of my longing for the romantic leads in particular nineties teen rom-coms. Devon Sawa, Joseph Gordon-Levitt, and Ethan Embry, with their shy smiles and twinkly eyes, tripping over themselves to make grand romantic gestures to the beautiful skinny girls they were in love with.

And then there was me: on the couch, eating Goldfish crackers, smeared in zit medication, wondering what it would feel like to be worthy of cinematic grand gestures. I thought I wasn't worthy, but I wanted it badly. That is, I wanted love. Also, I wanted to be worthy. And in my middle-school heart, these two concepts—love and worthiness—were dangerously intertwined.

Of course, it wasn't just movies. At school dances, at bar mitzvahs, everywhere I went, it seemed like everyone around me had somehow cracked the code. I'd barely mastered eye contact, and my friends were slow-dancing and holding hands and sometimes even kissing—which was a thing I thought about *constantly*. I practiced kissing my own arm—I actually did that—but it wasn't exactly to improve my skills for the real deal. It was an attempt to approximate what kissing felt like. I wasn't sure I'd ever get to try it out on someone else's lips.

Because I wasn't like the girls who slow-danced and held hands and kissed. I was quiet and earnest and pudgy. The other kids wore Abercrombie. I wore oversized nature-themed T-shirts and gym shorts in the summer, and turtleneck tunics all winter. My hair wouldn't stay in its ponytail, and I was always pushing up my glasses. Once a boy sat behind me in class and murmured *l-l-l-l-liposuction*. I saw a slam book once that voted me the "plainest" girl in seventh grade. I don't know if any of this sounds familiar to you, UL—I hope not—but I'm guessing you understand the feeling. Sir Shitstain made you understand the feeling. *Disgusting. Unworthy.*

6

High school was better, sort of. I never had one of those teen-movie-style transformations, but I was a bit more comfortable in my skin. For the first time in my life, I had friends who were boys. Sometimes I had crushes on them—achingly physical, intensely real, absolutely top secret. I'd joke around with them during the school day, and there was so much casual touching at play rehearsal . . . Romance didn't feel attainable, but sometimes it felt close. Sometimes I loved how it felt to want someone. I used to cry in my car when certain songs came on the radio. Every unrequited love song was about me. I felt very alive. I was constantly in love, but I could never say it out loud. I guess I didn't want to burden anyone by loving them. I guess I still felt unworthy.

Here's how the next part of the story should go: I go to college. I get confident. Either I kiss a million boys, or I stop caring about kissing. I'm brave and self-possessed and my goals are bigger and I'm better.

Here's how it actually goes: I go to college, and I've still never had a boyfriend, still never been kissed, still want it desperately. But sophomore year, I met a cute boy with glasses. We were at a party in my friend's dorm room. I remember sitting beside him on my friend's bed, talking like we were the only two people in the room. And I thought: *Maybe this is finally happening.* Maybe I've unlocked the secret.

I saw him around campus a few times in the following weeks. I learned his last name. I learned he was an English major and a writer. There was no Facebook back then, but I found him in the campus directory. I knew his email address, even though I was nowhere near brave enough to use it. But I was getting braver in other ways. I never used to confess my crushes, but I told my friends about this one. I said hi to him and smiled when I passed him between classes.

And I wrote an essay about him in a creative nonfiction writing class. It wasn't only about him. I didn't mention his name. But it was about that party and that feeling of connection and my hopefulness, even weeks later, and how I'd take the long way to class on Tuesdays and Thursdays, because I knew I'd run into him. It was about how I never knew the right thing to say or what to do with my hands, and it was about how those tiny moments could make or break my day. It was painfully honest, more so than I'd ever been. I didn't try to publish it or put it on the Internet—I would rather have died. But even submitting it to my professor was like handing over my heart.

The semester went on. I worked up the nerve to invite this boy to a party, and I'd obsessively rehearsed the whole encounter. I was still maneuvering to bump into him between classes, so that's when I planned to make my move. I'd mention the party casually, like I just happened to remember it. I'd ask for his email address—because I'd never let him know I'd already memorized it. Then, I'd forward him the info for the party, and when he showed up, I'd miraculously look like a nineties rom-com love interest. He'd ignore everyone else, and we'd talk for hours, just like the night we met. And then we'd kiss and have lingering eye contact, and he'd be my boyfriend. I'd have a *boyfriend.* And since *me with a boyfriend* was incomprehensible, there would obviously be some kind of transformation montage. I'd become the kind of girl who inspired grand romantic gestures. This was finally about to happen.

Anyway, I found him after class and asked him. Super casual, no big deal. *There's going to be a party. You should totally stop by.*

He was nice. I remember that. He smiled and told me the party sounded cool. He asked me to keep him in the loop about it.

And then he gave me the wrong email address.

It was a strange mistake for him to make. I knew people sometimes gave the wrong phone numbers on purpose to reject overly persistent suitors. But I didn't think I was overly persistent. For all my pining, I'd barely talked to this boy. And I'd structured the entire interaction so it wouldn't look like I was asking him out. *Of course* I wasn't asking him out. Not asking him out was my only move, really. I was the best at never putting myself out there, and I was the best at never getting rejected.

I didn't *think* I was being rejected.

It had to be a mistake. A rom-com moment. And wasn't it so like me to fall for a beautiful English major in glasses who couldn't remember his own email address?

I emailed him about the party. I used the correct email address, of course—the one he must have thought he'd given me. I even had a story ready to go, about how I got a Mailer Daemon from the email address he gave me—HILARIOUS, RIGHT—and only *then* did I look Mr. Mailer Daemon up in the campus directory. Of course. It's not like I'd ever think to look him up otherwise.

Anyway, he never wrote back. He also never showed up to the party.

A few days later, I ran into him outside my creative nonfiction classroom.

A few days after that, I learned he was my writing professor's teaching assistant, which means he'd read all my essays.

He'd read *that* essay.

To his credit, this boy never called me ugly. He never said I disgusted him. He was kinder than Sir Shitstain—but holy shit, did I feel ugly and disgusting. I finally got it. This boy didn't have any difficulty remembering his own email address. He was passively, politely rejecting me. I hated the thought of him pitying me—but even worse, I hated being something he had to *deal* with. My love was a burden, like I'd always suspected.

I was unworthy, like I'd always suspected.

You're a more generous person than me, UL, because you don't hate Sir Shitstain. I definitely hated Mr. Mailer Daemon. My best friend and I stopped speaking his name. We literally called him "The One We Hate." And, fifteen years later, I still cringe when I think of him. I especially cringe picturing him reading this letter. "*Jesus,*" he'll say. "This girl is writing about me again?"

Or maybe (probably, hopefully) he doesn't remember me at all.

My dearest UL: I'm so sorry to say you'll probably always remember Sir Shitstain. You may forget his face or even his name, but you'll remember how he made you feel. And I hate that. This kind of moment sears you. I wish it didn't. I also wish I could say this pain will make you stronger or braver, but I don't think that's true. There's nothing good or redemptive about what he did to you. And if there's a lesson there, he's the one who has to learn it. Not you.

But here's the good news: This experience doesn't need to be a lesson. It doesn't need to make you strong and brave. You're already strong and brave. So was I. We just can't always see it.

I'm thirty-four years old as I write this. I'm in love, and I'm married to the person I'm in love with. I have two children and a career I adore. I've held copies of my books in languages I can't read. I've visited the set of my book's movie adaptation. Do I feel unworthy sometimes? Absolutely yes. Am I confident and self-possessed? Not always. Not even usually. But I'm proud of what I've done and how the years have transformed me.

The years really have transformed me. I think the same thing will happen to you.

But here's the part that surprised me: Finding love wasn't the transformation. My first kiss didn't transform me. Neither did my first relationship, my first breakup, or my big summer wedding. The transformation wasn't even about me beginning to feel worthy—or, more importantly, understanding the difference between finding love and being worthy. I'm worthy now. I was worthy then. And I see that now, but that's not the thing I'm most proud of.

I'm proud that now, in my thirties, I'm finally talking about this. All of it: these feelings, these experiences, my insecurities, my shame, and the fierceness of my longing. Now when I write, I take my armor off first. Sometimes I write about people I love, and sometimes those people read what I write. It's never easy. It's terrifying. But I'm more proud of the honesty in my books than anything else about them. I'm proud of my honesty in my personal and professional relationships. I'm proud of my honesty on social media, and I'm proud of my honesty with myself. This is how I put my heart on the line. This is the way I know how to be brave.

And this is what you did in the letter you sent me. I'm in awe. You're sixteen years old. I know you think Sir Shitstain broke you, but you are so far from broken. You wrote to me, holding the door of your heart wide open. You amaze me. You inspire me.

You're so brave, and I love you.

Becky Albertalli

There's nothing stupid about wanting to be loved.
Believe me.

—*Everything Leads to You*, Nina LaCour

Dear Heartbreak,

I'm scared. I'm scared that something's wrong with me, or that people don't find me attractive or don't like me or something like that. I'm a senior in high school, and I've been in two relationships, one in ninth grade that was with a friend—we never actually ended up going on a date. The other was last year, and lasted a whopping three days. Besides that, no one's ever come up to me and asked me out, or told me that they like me, or even asked if I'd want to sit with them at lunch or something. A lot of my friends have had relationships before, even freshmen that I know are more experienced or lucky than me. I think I'm pretty, but I just don't know what is wrong with me that no one would want me. My mom tells me that things will be different in college, that I'll find someone there, but I'm so scared that it will be just like high school all over again. Last year for junior prom this other girl asked me to go with her, and asked me if I wanted to date her, too, and I said yes. She got a different girlfriend around a week later. I just want to know what's wrong with me, because I'm trying to do everything right, but nothing is working. I know that high school relationships usually don't work, but I at least wanted to try. I'm graduating in a couple weeks, and I've only ever been on one date. I know that things are supposed to get better, but I'm scared that nothing is going to change. I'm scared that I'm not good enough.

Love,

Scared, 17

GROW WILDLY

Dear Scared,

You are good enough.

I'll say it again, because I know that this statement is a tricky one to believe sometimes. So much around us and inside of us says, in so many overt and covert ways, that we are not. But believe me: You are good enough.

The summer after my senior year of high school, I worked in a bookstore. On weekend mornings, we would pick up giant thermoses of coffee from the café a few doors down so that our customers could sip while they browsed. It became my job to pick up the coffee, and when I walked into the café on my first morning shift, a cute boy just a little older than me was working there alone. He wore worn corduroy pants and hemp bracelets. He had a deep laugh and a slender body. He listened to music I'd never heard of. I remember wondering if he found me attractive. I remember thinking, *Will he choose me?* When he asked me out to dinner a few weeks later, I said yes. I rode in his car through the tunnel and over the bridge and into San

Francisco, lit up and brilliant on a Saturday night, and we sat across from each other at a Chinatown restaurant and made flirtatious, tentative conversation. And so we began.

It sounds familiar, right? A little like the plot of a predictable movie? It's what we picture for ourselves because we've been shown a million versions of it. We are tricked into thinking that this story is true for everyone, and then when it isn't true for us, we wonder why. You wanted this in high school—a person who would find you attractive, who would ask you out. I can feel the sadness in your letter—*your* sadness—and I want you to know that it's okay to grieve that high school relationship you didn't get to have. In all fairness, you *did* have a little bit—the thing with your friend in ninth grade, the three-day fling, an invitation to junior prom. These are more than what a lot of teenagers have by the time they finish high school. But still. You wanted something more than that. I'm sorry that you didn't get it.

Why don't you imagine it now, what it could have been like? Picture the person who would have asked you out. Maybe you two would have gone out on a proper date, to the movies or for ice cream in a park while you watched the sunset. Maybe you would have stayed out until your curfew, telling each other about yourselves. Maybe your first kiss would have been awkward at first and then passionate, and maybe you would have found ways to be at your houses when your parents were gone so that you could do more than kiss. You would have shown up at parties together, arms around each other. You would have slow-danced and made out in a corner. You would have taken up entire pages in each other's yearbooks. Or maybe you would have done none of these things—you're the only one who knows exactly what you wanted. Close your eyes and imagine it. Let it all play out.

It could have been really great.

Now, when you're ready, go ahead and let it go.

Scared, I want to tell you a secret. I've spent so much of my life trying to make myself a blank slate for other people. Nodding and smiling and saying yes. Waiting to be chosen. Wanting to be liked. Trying not to take up space, to never inconvenience, to read the mood of another person and alter my own to match them. I've spent so much of my life saying, "Me too," "It's up to you," "I really have no preference." The people who've grown to know me have done so *in spite* of this, not because of it. They've had to work harder. I know now that it's okay to be messy and difficult and angry and sad. It's okay to want things and to go after them. It's okay to end friendships or relationships that aren't working. It's okay to be inconvenient, to need something from someone and to ask for it. But it took me thirty-four years of living and a good therapist to get here. I still doubt myself far too often. I still marvel at how simple and true and freeing it is to say, "I disagree."

You may be wondering why I'm telling you all of this when you wrote with a straightforward problem of wanting someone to date. I'm sort of wondering the same thing. But at this point in my letter I need to confess that I did not face your particular struggle when I was younger, and I don't face it now, either. It wasn't the problem of not having someone to date that drew me to your letter, that made me think about you on my neighborhood walks and late at night while washing dishes and know that I needed to write you back. When I read your letter, one line stood out to me more than any of the others: "I'm trying to do everything right, but nothing is working." I read it, and I read it again, and I worried over how much of *you* you must be erasing, how much of *you* you must be holding back, in your effort to do everything right. What do you love, Scared? What ideas fill you with wonder? Do you like to paint, or collect things, or play video games, or try out YouTube tutorials? Do you read novels, or go on hikes, or speak another language? When you and your friend fooled around in ninth grade, how did you like to be kissed? I am the kind of person who, when I want something badly, finds it difficult to pay attention to anything else. I get the feeling that you might be like that, too. That you might be postponing your happiness while you wait for someone to choose you.

Since I was thirteen years old, I have been in a relationship. I don't think I went more than six months without one. And I know that to you, who craves romantic connection, this might sound lucky. But it means that all the growing up I did, all the learning about myself, and the figuring out who I wanted to be, was done in relation to another person. That comes with its comforts and it comes with its challenges. It often means that when you're struggling with yourself, you jab an elbow into the eye of the person who loves you. It means that when you're navigating the storms of your own heart, you break someone else's in the process.

Which brings me back to that boy from the café. We had our first date in the city and I tried to act like the kind of girl he'd want to be on a date with, but since I didn't know him yet, I didn't know what that kind of girl she would be. I feared that I was boring. I worried over whether he'd kiss me and I didn't know if I wanted him to or not. He didn't on that first date but he did on the next one. It turns out that we had both been worried and nervous in our own ways. He was sweet and smart and I was lonely. We dated for longer than we should have—well into my second year of college. He had a crush on another girl.

I did, too.

I don't want to tell you the story of *how* I met her. I want to tell the story of how it *felt*. Like the crowded room we were in became silent but for her. Like she moved in slow motion. Like every time she exhaled, I breathed a little of her in. I learned her name from a roll sheet our professor sent up and down the aisles. I learned what her voice sounded like from the smart things she said in class. I learned what it felt like to want a specific person so badly—to be so drawn to someone—that once the semester was over I never walked anywhere on campus without searching for her. I had memorized her face from countless stolen glances and one fortuitous group work session when we ended up together and I fought through my shyness to talk to her. Even after months had passed since our class had ended, I knew her face well enough to draw it. I sketched her in pencil, and then I carried the drawing of her in my journal as though it were a photograph she'd given to me. The drawing was a wish. And when, a full year later, we had a weekly class together in her very last semester of college, that wish was granted.

I ended things with the boy because all I could think of was the girl. I was still too shy to make a move, so I enlisted the help of my friends and slowly, she gravitated to our section of the classroom. Every day that wasn't Thursday I spent counting down to it. Every Thursday morning before class began I tried on all my clothes, or went to the mall next to campus to find something that would make her choose me. I casually mentioned a show I was going to and asked if she wanted to come, my heart pounding. She couldn't, but she smiled every time she looked at me. Finally we started hanging out outside of class, zipping through the city in her little red car. We went to parks and restaurants and bookstores and record stores and I kept waiting for her to choose me. I hadn't figured out how to tell her. Meanwhile, more than one of her ex-girlfriends wanted her back. They called and cried to her on the phone. The boy she was best friends with was in love with her. He showed up at a restaurant where we were having lunch one day, desperation in his every gesture. I had been waiting and waiting for her to choose me but I was afraid I was going to wait for so long that I'd miss my chance. So I gathered every bit of courage I had and I told her how I felt in clumsy words that were the best that I could do. They were clumsy, yes, but they got the message across, and I remember the light of understanding flick on in her eyes. She smiled and said, *"Oh,"* her voice soft and surprised. A few days later, when she picked me up, there was no ambiguity: We were on a date.

Scared, it's impossible to do everything right. Be kind to yourself—stop trying. Even at our best, we are messy and complicated beings. We are stupid and petty and mean and boring and gross. What you *should* try is to be fully yourself. Maybe in the past you would have gone out with anyone who asked you. Maybe all you needed was *someone*, and anyone could have been that person—the more-than-friend who never took you out, the fickle girl who asked but didn't follow through—but here's the thing: You get to choose who you want to be with. You get to do the asking, too. There is no guarantee that they will say yes, but the simple, brave act of putting yourself out there will transform you.

For every gross part of us, there is a beautiful part. I understand how badly you want to share that with someone. And I understand how, when you don't have anyone to share yourself with, you worry that something is wrong, when really, most likely, it just isn't the right place or the right time.

What I'm trying to tell you is this: When that slow-motion moment comes, and you feel the air being sucked out of the room, and you can't take your eyes off someone—take a risk and talk to them. Or even if it isn't that dramatic—if there's someone smart or cute or interesting, if there's someone you feel like kissing—ask that person out. And in the absence of those feelings, don't sit still, waiting to be chosen. Don't feel like your life is on hold or missing a piece because you aren't dating anyone. These are the times you can grow wildly and with abandon, knowing you won't jab anyone in the eye or break anyone's heart. These are the times to perfect your French accent, or watch every Greta Garbo film, or learn to play the ukulele. These are the times to figure out what you want to major in, to immerse yourself in ideas, to go on adventures with friends or strangers, to find out who you are by discovering what you thrive on.

The girl I fell for in college? We're married now. We have a daughter and a little green house and tomatoes growing in our garden. I catch myself often in moments of wonder that I could have the kind of love that I do. It's as magnificent as you hope it will be. When it comes to you, it will be worth all the disappointment that came before it.

But, Scared, let me tell you this: The best love story is the one where you love yourself.

Wishing you many kinds of love,
and wild growth and courage,
and all the lessons I've learned much sooner,

Nina LaCour

Well, right now it's feeling worse because the same thoughts are repeating themselves, bouncing around in there. You're like a teakettle begging to let out some steam. You need to let someone pull you off the stove and pour you into a cup.

—*Let's Get Lost*, Adi Alsaid

Dear Heartbreak,

I am afraid that someone will love me (or think they will) only to find out once they get to know me that I am truly not a person they could love. I feel like I must keep people at a distance to protect not only myself, but them as well. It is so lonely and so heartbreaking because I do not know how to fix it. I wish I could because I truly do love others, but now I am so isolated I don't even know where I could go to even meet people. I still have hope, though, that someday things can change for the better.

—Motionless, 19

DO YOU CARE TO RESIDE WITHIN?

Dear Motionless,

How much do you know about truffles? I knew some of the basics before writing to you—rare fungi, found in the dirt, used in cooking—but I wanted to do a little research before answering you. Here's what I learned:

- It's believed that they evolved underground to protect themselves from forest fires, frost, and other environmental threats.
- Truffles form part of a symbiotic relationship with a host tree; each provides the other with crucial nutrients.
- It's not just pigs that find them; trained dogs and goats do, too.
- A truffle once sold for over $37,000.
- In 2016, France harvested approximately 55 tons of truffles.

I think you may know where I'm going here, but it'll do you no good for me to be vague. Motionless, you are a truffle. You have sent yourself underground for protection, to hide from the harm of heartbreak and the soul-crushing frost of being unloved. This, in a very real and natural sense, is a perfectly reasonable approach to life. Seek safety from harm.

But it sounds to me that you know that's not how you want to live your life. You have this self-awareness, and you have hope. These are good starts. Now ask yourself this: Is protection from pain worth living underground? Will the benefits of exposure to the outside world outweigh the potential harms that will come your way?

Truffles hide in the dirt, but attract a host of animals. Mainly humans, who've found that even a fungus hidden in the ground is worth searching for. For any of what I say next to work, though, you have to think of yourself as a truffle. You have to know that you are inherently valuable. If no one is saying that to you, you have to say it to yourself.

You have to be kind to yourself. The assumption that someone could get to know you and then find you completely unlovable, well, it's a typically human assumption. It's a damn rude way to act toward ourselves, but most of us do it at some point or another. You're not alone in the fear. Like everyone else, though, you're wrong, and you have to move past it.

I used to be a shy kid, stuck within a proverbial shell. I fostered dreams of showing my true, goofy self to the world, but kept it hidden from most people. My sister jokes that until I came back from a trip to Israel when I was eighteen, she'd never heard me speak a word.

I'm not sure why I felt the need to hide. Maybe, like you, it was a fear that people would not appreciate the person I would reveal myself to be. I searched through my old LiveJournal account (a sort of early 2000s Tumblr) and found a bevy of angsty posts, sparked through with moments of joy on days when I did feel comfortably myself. I wrote love letters to girls in high school and then fled before they could respond, thinking the move was inherently pathetic. If I recall correctly, I once even referred to myself as pathetic within the letter, casting myself as unworthy of love.

My brother puts it this way: "You couldn't decide if you cared or not. Then you decided you didn't."

He said this when we shared an apartment in college, when I was doing things like taking spontaneous road trips to Baker, California, just to have lunch, or founding a student organization at UNLV called Students for the Advancement of Silliness. I brought my first girlfriend to the top floor of a library and rained down thirty notecards with book quotations on them. I wrote editorials in the school newspaper about choosing to be happier. I broke out of my proverbial shell, deciding, as my brother pointed out, that I no longer cared to reside within it.

It's a damn hard step to implement, I know. Insecurities and worry and maybe experiences with others have wired your brain in a way that has turned you mean toward yourself. Try to catch instances of this happening. I was guilty of this plenty of times on that museum of myself I found on the Internet. Any time you start thinking that there's nothing lovable about you, argue with yourself. Stick up for yourself to that shitty inclination we all have inside. Remind yourself of how much love you have for others. How you are selfless, a good cook, patient, smart, kind, charitable, a champion cuddler—fill in the blanks, whatever they may be. And if you are right now thinking that you can't fill in the blanks, that's the mean part of your brain and I want it to shut up. Take a long, *kind* look at yourself. Assess yourself with only positive words. Say these words out loud until you believe them.

I happen to think that, eventually, a pig or dog or goat or human who finds value in you will find you anyway. Truffles are delicious; that's why we seek them out. I don't think you *want* to wait around for that to happen, but it's something I've found to be true in life. It takes time. In high school and in college, I found groups of friends that were merely company, and I found people who saw me for who I am and loved me for it. Patience isn't my recommended strategy, but it's good to keep in mind. The people who value you come around. It doesn't always feel that way, but they're out there, searching for you, just like you should be searching for them.

Will some of them get close to you and then later find that you are not what they were searching for? Absolutely. Motionless, it's going to happen. Just not every time. We meet people in life with whom we are incompatible. No matter how great truffles are on French fries, shaved onto pasta and risotto, there are people who dislike them. Our differences are sometimes obvious right away, and sometimes they only come to light after a while, leading to heartbreak and pain and the desire to burrow in the dirt. This doesn't mean we are universally unlovable. If someone gets to know who you are and decides not to be in your life, it is not an admonishment of who you are; it does not diminish your inherent value. Quite frankly, screw those people. You don't want them in your life anyway. Wait for the truffle lovers.

Now let's talk about that second bullet point, the host tree that depends on you. You're feeling overwhelmed by loneliness, so it probably doesn't feel like you have one right now. But I promise you there's a larger community that you need and that needs you. I recommend you look for it, a tiny root at a time.

Maybe you've hidden yourself away from the roots that are already there, or maybe you've yet to find them. A coworker who counts on your interaction every day. A classmate who admires the things you say in class and aspires to be as thoughtful as you. Your cat, who counts on you for food and for the love you provide it even though it never seems to return the favor. You belong in the world, Motionless, even if you've buried yourself in the ground, even if you feel apart from it. Look for the small ways this is already true, and treat them like ropes cast down to save you and slowly pull yourself up to the surface.

Let's set aside the poetics and the pep talk, and dispense with some practical advice on where to meet people: couchsurfing.com. Even if you don't travel, the people that use the site are by and large lovely, good-hearted people, social in a way that embraces those who aren't normally social. When I moved to Monterey, California, to start writing, I didn't know a single person in the area. I posted on Couchsurfing once, and within a day I was meeting up with a guy for coffee. He introduced me to a whole social group who would be my closest friends during my time there, as well as hooked me up with a volunteer job at an elementary school so that my visa could remain current. There were potlucks where I spent a whole night eating, talking travel, feeling like people who were previously strangers could easily whittle away my loneliness. Look for meet-ups in your town. There are subgroups for people who share your interests. Try meetup.com, too, where you can find everything from language-exchange buddies and book clubs to people looking to climb a mountain or develop an app.

Volunteer somewhere relevant to your interests. An urban garden, maybe. Something to do with kids, if you're interested in spending time with innocent, maddening, amusing, filterless little human beings. A library, to surround yourself with books and the people who love them.

Two years after returning to Mexico, I was living at home with my parents and had not much in the way of a social circle. Writing is a wonderful job, but it can be a lonely, isolating affair, and I was desperate to find a way to have people in my life again. I thought about jobs that I could get that would allow me to still write, but that were within my interest level, so I applied to be a flight attendant, and then a basketball coach.

I was hired for the latter, and the changes were almost immediate. It took a while for me to really find my people within the school where I was coaching, because, again, that's sometimes just how life is. But eventually I found them. They found me. Working at that school led to my meeting some of the closest friends I've ever had, including my soon-to-be wife.

These acts of reaching out will probably be a little bit outside of your comfort zone. Do them anyway. Your comfort zone is malleable. Just like it's shrunk in around you, you can make it grow. Don't go thinking you've buried yourself in the dirt forever. The more you push back against your comfort zone, the more you put yourself in an opportunity to dig yourself out and find the people who will appreciate you for exactly who you are.

When I started Students for the Advancement of Silliness, I had to be outgoing, show my weird self to a much wider world than my close group of friends. I had to file paperwork with the university, had to organize events, though I'm the kind of person that practically flees from plans. It was uncomfortable, and at times it didn't feel like there was a point to it. But again, that move brought people close to me, the exact kind of people who would appreciate who I am.

When you've met new people this way, I think it's helpful to remember that France harvested 55 tons of truffles in 2016. You are not the only truffle out there. Some may not be part of your host tree, and some may come to harm you, but many know exactly what it's like to feel what you're feeling now. We're all truffles, hidden in some sort of dirt, waiting to nourish and be nourished.

Remember that there are pigs out there who know how valuable you are. Remember that the benefits of an exposed life outweigh the harms. Remember to be kind to yourself, Motionless.

Cara takes my hand in hers and holds it on top of her stomach. Our heads are near, on the same large pillow, and every once in a while, when we breathe in at the same time, our shoulders touch. I almost cry a little, because I never think anyone wants to be this close to me.

—*37 Things I Love*, Kekla Magoon

Dear Heartbreak,

I think I'm alone. I'm surrounded by people, but I'm alone. I try to fit in, but I just . . . can't. I'm a thirteenth wheel. I still have my family, but they're drifting apart, slowly but surely. At the same time, I can call people and they almost always answer, but I feel like a pest. Just for once, I would like to BE called. If you have any advice, I would appreciate it.

Thanks,

N

IF YOU CALL, I WILL ANSWER

Dear N,

Alone.

That word on the page looks exactly how it feels—like standing all by yourself in a very white room. Nothing on the walls. No furniture, no windows.

Sometimes that room is your own mind.

Is it an endless room? One you can walk and walk through? Or is it a tight little box, in which you can barely stretch your arms to their full length?

Alone.

This feeling has nothing to do with the volume of people around you. It sounds like you have a group of friends, maybe as many as twelve of them. You're certainly not the first human being to feel less than satisfied, even in good company. We are, universally, made of more than the sum of our parts. Each one of us is an ocean, rich with unseen depths.

It hurts to feel unseen. To feel unappreciated. It hurts when you don't fit in. Humans are social creatures. We crave company and contact, the warmth of other bodies, other hearts.

And yet, we are so often by ourselves.

Alone.

This word likes its capital A. The sharpness of it, the certainty. It says, fuck you, world, I'm the Eiffel Goddamn Tower— look at me against the sunset sky and kneel as you were always meant to.

Most of us don't want to kneel. Most of us don't want to live forever in the state of Alone. We want to reach out, we want to be reached. The saddest thing I can imagine is a person who lived an entire human life and never felt connected to anyone.

In the end, most of us don't end up living forever completely Alone. And chances are, N, you won't, either. The world is full of interesting people. Somehow, against all odds, we find each other. There may be deep loves, rich friendships, and a new, stronger meaning of family yet to come for you. Not immediately, but the best things in life are worth waiting for.

If you're rolling your eyes right now, I don't blame you. Promises and hopes for the future mean very little when you're in pain. The hard truth is—Alone is a feeling that may always be with you. Albeit to different degrees. In this life, we are inextricably bound to our own minds, our own skin. We barely have time to get to know ourselves deeply, let alone to have others know us. Parts of us may well be unknowable.

It doesn't mean we shouldn't try. And you are trying, N. The best news in your letter comes in this line: "I can call people, and they almost always answer."

Even though it doesn't feel like it, you are well on your way to feeling less alone. The first step to getting called is to KEEP ON CALLING. Be gentle and thoughtful in your reaching out, but try to be unafraid. One of the hardest things to do is to put yourself out there, to be vulnerable to the possible rejection you fear most. To call someone you like when you aren't sure they'll pick up or you're afraid they'll think you're a pest, takes great courage. It makes me smile to imagine you nervously picking up the phone. In my life I have rarely been brave like that.

I write this letter to you from a ditch on the side of a road in rural Pennsylvania. I've run my car off the road trying to avoid a deer, and I can't get it back out on my own. So I'm waiting. I'm a little shaken and a little scared, and I'm in the middle of nowhere so I don't know whether help will arrive before dark. I don't have anyone to call, apart from my insurance agent, and her cool, businesslike sympathy is not what I want in my ear. I want someone who loves me to wish me back home. Someone who would be willing to talk to me while I wait, or to offer to leap into a car and drive a hundred miles to come get me, however irrational that would be. But I don't have that person. I don't have anyone to call, and the tow truck is on its way, so I might as well do my writing. I'm uninjured and my laptop still works, and as I was driving I'd already been thinking about what to say to you, and how to explain the joys and sorrows of being—or feeling—Alone.

There is a great sadness to Alone. There is also strength. There is strength in being of yourself and doing for yourself. But you cannot give in to it, or resign yourself to it. You cannot become afraid to keep trying. You cannot become afraid to keep calling.

I sit here, cross-legged in the dirt in the middle of this one-lane road, thinking about all the ridiculous things I've done by myself because I was too embarrassed or too scared to ask for help. I dragged a sleeper sofa down a flight of stairs once. I've built countless IKEA furniture pieces that are supposed to require "team lifting." I've driven myself to the hospital with a broken foot. I've moved a 40-gallon fish tank multiple times. I've stayed in hotels because I was too shy to ask a friend to stay over, or I worried that they'd feel unnecessarily obligated to take me in even if they didn't want to. I've done this more than once, only to receive a sad message days later: "Why didn't you tell me you were in town?"

The answer, almost always, is "Because I was scared."

I don't want to live my life in fear. There is a certainty in Aloneness. No one can tell you what to do, what to watch, what to wear. You get to make all the choices. You never have to compromise. There is plenty of uncertainty in Alone, too. I would like someone to alert me when I have spinach in my teeth. I would like to be able to tell the joke that occurs to me when that particular Downy commercial comes on. I would like to tell my joke, and have someone there to laugh. Is it really so much to ask to not be all alone?

I sit here, slightly shell-shocked, and I find myself wanting to call someone. Today, I find my courage by thinking of you, N. I wonder if you feel it from afar, a burst of a feeling that is softer than Alone. Probably not, right? I don't have your number and so I can't call you. I can only tell you, long after the fact, that thinking about you gave me more courage than usual.

I called my friend Emily from the side of the road. I pushed down the knowledge that I was probably interrupting her dinner with her wife. I called anyway.

Guess what? She answered.

Guess what else? For those few minutes, I felt less Alone.

Okay, N. A few hours have passed and I'm safe and warm and fed and able to charge my laptop. (All the important things.) Having some distance from my moment of crisis helped me see that I was never as alone as I thought. I figured out who else to call, and kind friends came to the roadside to wait for the tow truck with me. They helped me ask the right questions and rescue my belongings. My friend Nicole, who lives a hundred miles away, offered to come get me, and I started to cry.

When you have a bad day, a bad week, a bad *moment*, however long it lasts, it is easy to lose perspective. I don't know if you've had a significant crisis in your life yet, but when you do, watch who shows up. Make note of who you most want to call and how they respond. We don't form our closest friendships in a vacuum. We forge them in the fires of adversity, as we walk hand in hand through the valley of despair.

For a long time, I believed I needed to be as perfect as possible in order to get people to like me. Good behavior had been drilled into me as a child, and I learned to equate such behavior with respect and affection. The version of myself that I performed in order to be seen as a responsible student, a good daughter, a polite young woman in the eyes of the adult world . . . that performative self only allowed a small part of me to be revealed. I believed that you had to behave a certain way to be good and to be liked, and this belief messed with my head. I hid the things about me that were weird, because I wanted to fit in. I tried so hard to be normal that I made myself bland. I missed out on a whole great nerdy and quirky subculture that would have resonated deeply with me. I was too afraid to let my freak flag fly, and, as a result, I probably missed some opportunities to befriend similar freaks. I didn't find the friends who really GET me until late in college and in my early twenties. As I get older, I continue to become better at being ME, and that is what helps draw the right kinds of people to me. Most amazingly, some of these people are actually people I knew and hung out with in high school, but we have all become more OURSELVES and grown closer. Some of us grew apart for the same reasons, but that's okay. I'm left with something better.

If you don't quite fit in with the people you know, think about why that might be the case. Why do you feel that way? Do you really like these friends? Do you have some things in common, but not everything? That's actually all right. Most of us need a lot of different kinds of friends to fill all the corners of our hearts.

I spent a long time assuming that the longer I knew people, the closer we would become. I believed that our friendships would deepen automatically. This is true to an extent. Another piece, though, is finding the right friends. People that you click with. It can take time to find those people. It can take a little bit of searching.

Think about the handful of people you genuinely like best and want to spend time with. Invite those friends to hang out. Think about what you have in common and what would be fun for both (or all) of you. There's nothing wrong with being the one who calls!

My problem is so often the opposite. I get too afraid to call people or to invite them over. I get so convinced that they don't really like me or wouldn't want to hear from me. I don't really even know why I feel this way. There are a lot of things I like about myself. I'm creative, I'm funny. I'm thoughtful, I'm caring, I'm smart. Other people should like these things about me, too. And many people do. I no longer expect EVERYONE to like me, and I no longer go out of my way to try to win anyone's affection. It's very freeing, to simply be myself and do my best and HOPE that the right people will notice me and respond. When I'm left by myself, which happens quite often, I find ways to celebrate myself and remind myself of my best qualities, because it's important to know.

Alone doesn't have to mean lonely. There are plenty of things to love and appreciate about yourself while you're waiting to build deeper connections with others. What are your best attributes? How can you enjoy your own company? Your relationship with self is as important as relationships with friends and family. What do YOU like about YOU? What is your safe space? What is the best part about Alone? The part you can stand?

The thing is, we never fully know how other people feel about us. Self-doubt and insecurity are cruel little brain buddies. They can convince you that your best friend, who just invited you to a sleepover, doesn't *really* want to hang out with you. Sometimes you have to use logic to override the emotional fears and awkwardness. Remind yourself that people like you. Remind yourself what is most likable about yourself. Don't let yourself forget.

I understand your fear about being a pest when you reach out to your friends. I happen to be an introvert and very skittish. I fail at this test more often than I succeed, by resisting the impulse to call someone when I want to. I don't carry a lot of regrets about my life, but the main one is not telling people how I feel. Not telling them that I care. Not calling. To me, dear N, it sounds like you're well on your way to a happier place. You are braver than I have often been. You *call*.

It's entirely possible that some of your friends are more like me—too shy or nervous to reach out. Maybe YOU are the strong one; maybe YOU are the one helping other people feel less Alone.

I know how you feel, N. I want to be called. I want to feel chosen, and cared for. I don't want to chase anyone's affection. That's a good way to be; that takes strength. It means I'm not diving into a bad situation simply because I'm desperate for someone, anyone, to like me. But relationships are a two-way street. The way to get called is to keep calling. The way to get called is to continue to forge bonds with other people, inch by inch. Let them see you vulnerable. Let them see what you need and who you are. They will begin to reveal themselves to you, too.

Sometimes the thing that makes you feel most alone is having someone that you want to reach out to, but your mind convinces you that they will not want to hear from you. That you're a "pest." The feeling of being alone in a crowd is so much worse than being alone on your own. Your mind can play tricks on you, try to convince you that you're not fun, or funny, or clever, or interesting. Why would anyone want to hang out with you, anyway?

Tell your mind to STOP BEING SO NEGATIVE. It sounds easy on paper, but it may not be that easy in real life. It takes time to develop confidence in social situations, and we all make mistakes. We say the wrong thing or we leave an awkward voice mail, or we text one too many times and slightly annoy someone. The good news is: A true friend who is worthy of your time and energy will understand and forgive that kind of mistake. Humans are flawed and relationships are messy. If we don't take any risks, we never get to the good part of relationships—which is being flawed and messy together, and finding joy in the things that are wrong with all of us.

I wish I could give you a miracle cure. I wish I could tell you it gets a thousand times better. Alone is not the sort of thing that goes away.

Most of all, I wish I could tell you that you are not alone. Sometimes you are. Sometimes we all are.

What I can tell you is, the moments when I've been brave enough to make the call, the moments when I've been bold enough to kick over the Eiffel Tower—these have become some of my finest moments. In my weakness, I find strength. In my fear, I find courage. In the depths of Alone, when I stretch out my hand, I always find something to hold on to.

Kekla

I'm like everyone else in this stupid, bloody, amazing world. I'm flawed. Impossibly so. But hopeful. I'm still me.

—*The Sweet Far Thing*, Libba Bray

Dear Heartbreak,

There are many days where I wonder why nobody has ever liked me in the ways that some have liked my best friends. I am a virgin in every way. The only date that I have been on was prom and I asked him, not the other way around. I have a disease that I feel has really hindered my chances of finding any type of romantic love. I have had heartbreak, but it has come from other things. My parents met when they were in middle school and were high school sweethearts. I have always wanted a love like that, that would last almost three decades, but I am at the end of my first year of college and nothing has happened in that department.

This year has been harder than most because I lost my first dog and one of our cats. It was the first time that I had ever really felt the pain of losing a beloved pet and I just felt so broken because our dog was one of the only beings who ever hung out with me and loved me unconditionally and it was just so hard letting him go. I just miss him so much. I do know that he is in a better place but I will always have this huge hole in my heart that will take a long while to really fill back up.

There have been a few boys in my life who I thought could be a boyfriend, but now I see that it might not have been the best time for me to have one. The first one was someone that I met in the third grade and we connected through our love of

Harry Potter. When I had one of my more scarring surgeries he pretended like Daniel Radcliffe had signed this poster that my classmate had made for me since I was going to be missing a few weeks of school. I was so touched that he had done that. We would talk in middle school and high school but we drifted apart and I've always hated that. There was one guy in fifth grade who I knew would never be into me just because it was fifth grade and there couldn't have been anything between us. I wrote a fairy-tale story with us being the main characters and I read it out aloud to the class and I was so embarrassed. The last thing that I vividly remember about this boy is that he hit me in the back of the head with a basketball as I was walking onto my bus. Another one was a guy that I knew in middle school who was in a class with me. He was one of the cutest guys in our grade and I had asked my best friend to ask him if he had any feelings for me. Obviously he didn't. Most of the guys were idiots in that school, but he was one of the nicer ones. There were some guys in high school that I had crushes on, but it really never went anywhere.

I have also had heartbreak with friends. There was this one girl who I had been friends with forever and she was getting too toxic for me. She would keep ditching me for other girls in our grade. I have always wondered if it was because of my disease or something. I can't drive because of my eyesight and I have always wondered if I could drive if it would have helped at all. I do have this great guy friend who I met through a support group for teens with chronic illnesses. He was the one I invited to prom and we had the best time at two proms. How many girls could say that they were able to go to two proms? He is really like the brother that I never had. He is one of my best friends and I wouldn't change a thing about our relationship.

My questions are:

- Why are there people who seem to find love so early in their lives but there are others who search for it their whole lives and never seem to find it?
- Is it okay to wear your heart on your sleeve all the time or should you close yourself off?
- How much of yourself should you let show when meeting someone you might like the first time?

Thank you for this opportunity,
Hoping for a Chance @ Love, 19

WE HAVE TO BE WHO WE ARE

Dear Hoping for a Chance @ Love,

Let me start by saying that I am so, so sorry about the loss of your beloved pets. Of course you feel devastated and heartbroken. That's because you have the capacity to love and be loved in return. Pets *do* love us unconditionally. It's only natural to mourn their passing and miss that burrowing-our-faces-in-their-faces kind of all-good love when it is gone. I'm so sorry.

Guarding against pain is something we humans do, in all sorts of ways, and I hear that fear of additional loss lurking here in your letter, dear Hoping. Loss of friends. Loss of potential boyfriends. Loss of pride in the face of rejection. Loss of love before it begins. There's so much to talk about here, and I hope it's okay if I take my time.

To have a chronic illness is tough. I don't know, of course, precisely the nature of your disease, and so I would not presume to understand what you struggle with daily. I can only relate to you, one human to another, heart-to-heart. You have been open and honest with me; I promise to respond with openness and honesty in return. And so, I will say that I do know from my own experience having been disfigured after a car accident at eighteen and losing my eye, what it is to feel different or apart from others because of that experience. I know what it is to have harbored fears that somehow my "differentness" hindered my chances at romantic love and friendship, just as you wonder about it now. (I, too, cannot drive due to vision issues, by the way. We would make for a fun road-trip pair: "I thought you were driving." "Dude, I thought YOU were driving." "Where's the car?" "Dunno. Can't see it." "Yeah, me either.")

I hope you're okay with really irreverent humor, Dear Hoping for a Chance. Honestly, a sense of humor has seen me through heartbreak more times than I can count. And it has been a better companion than some dates.

More on that shared sensibility to come, but first, let's talk about boys and being dateless. Mind if I sit next to you on this bench in the park, dear Hoping? (I have imagined us in a lovely park setting. It is late spring. The weather is perfect—warm with a breeze. There are ducks. But they are far enough away that they won't bother us. Ducks, while fluffy and cute, are actually big biters. See? Nothing is perfect. Anyway . . .) You were a virgin all through high school? Dude! Me too! Here. Have some popcorn. (In this fantasy park, we have buttered popcorn. It's amazing. People wish they were us. Who can blame them?)

Even before my accident, I spent a decent portion of my high school years wondering why I was so dateless when almost all of my friends got asked out on the regular. I mean, I showered every day. I was not totally unpopular. I had, to the best of my knowledge, never turned to a guy and said in a demonic voice, "Upon our first kiss, I will rip your beating heart from your chest with my bare hands and devour it, thus granting me immortal life while banishing your soul to an everlasting hell-scape where they do not even have fries. Mwahahahaha!" Pretty sure that never happened.

But the gentlemen? They were not inclined to dial my digits. Like, *ever*. I remember having a massive crush on this boy named Greg. One day, he asked me if I wanted to go to an art museum in Fort Worth to see a photography exhibit. *This was it! My glorious Technicolor dream date had arrived at last!* While we walked through the museum, tilting our heads in unison as we examined black-and-white, postwar French photographs, I kept waiting for him to ask me out. And when he said, "Hey, Libba, there's something I really wanted to ask you . . ." I was so glad I'd put on lip gloss and mascara because, whoa! This was going to be epic. Until he confessed that he had a wicked crush on my BFF: "I was wondering if you could help me get a date with her?" Girl. That long ride home SUCKED. I sat in the car with this demented, frozen smile on my face while my heart seized on the floorboard like a dying fish gasping for air. This was not the first nor the last time this happened. It seemed like I was always the friend. The confidante. The match-maker. But never the girl that made them go weak-kneed. Never the girlfriend. I began to wonder if there was just something about me that spelled doom in the love department.

When prom rolled around, no one asked me. I ended up going through a date arranged by a high school friend. It went down in the girls' bathroom kind of like this:

Her: "Hey, Libba, I heard you don't have a date to the prom."

Me: "No, I don't." (Good to know my dateless status IS EXCITING NEWS FOR ALL!)

Her: "I'm going with a boy from Jesuit in Dallas, but my parents will only let me go if I double-date. If I can find somebody for you, will you go?"

If I can find somebody for you. A date had to be found for me! *Duuude.* I felt like a sad TV commercial. "For just pennies a day, you can fund a prom date for this poor, hideous girl and keep her from a night of skin-clearing masks and mindless Doritos eating. Won't you make a donation today?" I admit, I had to get over the wound to my pride. No one had asked me to prom, and now I was going, but it wasn't the sort of romantic lovefest that all the teen romance movies had promised me. It was a charity date, to my mind. The date in question, a super-nice guy named Chris, showed up in a tux and red Converse high-tops, and I thought, yeah, this'll definitely work.

If this were a Hollywood movie, he and I would've fallen in love over the course of that night, probably while also fighting crime. Didn't happen. We had a great time with zero pressure. I never saw him again, and that was perfectly okay. Mostly what I remember about that night was that I saw the new video for the Tom Tom Club's "Genius of Love," which I had more love for than any boy. (Meanwhile, my BFF had gone to prom with one of our high school's total stud muffins, a guy with perfectly feathered hair who cleared the dance floor so that we could all witness his signature splits-and-back-up smooth move. She had been crazy excited about the date, certain that it was the start of an epic romance, only to realize during the long night that he was only using her to get back at his ex-girlfriend. I'm just saying, my dear Hoping: Sometimes, what looks like perfection on the surface turns out to be a real shit sandwich underneath, and the stuff you don't even see coming, those beautiful happy accidents, turn out to be the best of times.)

Okay. Can I whisper this to you, dear Hoping? No one is listening but you, me, and the ducks. The real-deal truth is, I'm not so sure I was really ready for a boyfriend. I wanted things out of life. Things that were about me first. It's just that I had absorbed so many messages about what I was "supposed" to want versus what I actually wanted, that I didn't quite trust myself on this score. While my friends talked about getting boys' attention, going on dates, love, and sex, I nodded along while thinking, "Yeahhh, I want it, but that sounds like . . . a lot of work?" My secret fear was that a boyfriend would require a lot of care and feeding when I was already trying to learn how to take care of myself. I wanted out of my small, dead-end-feeling town. I wanted to have grand adventures, see far-off places, meet new people. I had one foot out the door. I didn't know this on a conscious level. It was something that lurked in the deep of me, like an electric eel, slithering about in the dark unconscious where such things swim. I wanted more. Maybe you do, too.

Also, for what it's worth? Being nineteen is damn hard. At nineteen, you're crossing over into real adulthood—a whole new decade—and it's fraught with saying goodbye to adolescence while still having no idea what to expect next. It's like you're the protagonist in a vaguely dystopian, somewhat comic novel in which you also pay rent. Honestly, it gets better. I promise. Nineteen is just . . . Oh, man. Here, have some more popcorn. Have some M&Ms, too.

Now. Dear Hoping, let's talk about what it is to go through this world feeling as if there is something about you that keeps you alone. You say, "I have a disease that I feel has really hindered my chances of finding any type of romantic love." That was the line in your letter that pierced me to the heart. Again, I make no presumptions about the particulars of your struggle, but I do know this awful feeling, this fear, all too well, my sweet. I often wondered if the reason I didn't date like all of my friends was because I had a messed-up face with a wonky eye that didn't move. I spent years feeling ugly and weird and different. Not "normal." Whatever the hell that means. And I assumed I would never find love because of it. My secret refrain was, "What's wrong with me?" I wish I could spare you the unnecessary pain of this feeling, which is such a lie. If I could have a wish for you, my sweet Hoping for a Chance, it's that instead of asking,

"What's wrong with me?" you might instead think about all that is right with you and nurture it.

You deserve more. Trust me on this.

I was twenty-one when I had my first true love. We dated for a year, and then that summer, we were separated. He went home to Arizona to work with his father, and I went home to have a big surgery, one of the many I endured after my accident. This one was a bone graft in which they removed a rib plus cartilage from my ears in order to make me a new eye socket, cheekbone, and nose. What nobody told me beforehand was that this surgery isn't exact. Bone shrinks over time, so they kind of have to guess and overshoot to start, which meant that my face was swollen and asymmetrical for nearly a year afterward. Some of the bone was uneven (it still is), and my fake eye looked stranger than usual. I was horribly self-conscious and worried: What if, when I saw my boyfriend at the end of the summer, he didn't like the way I looked? What if he thought I was ugly?

Dear Hoping, the day I went to pick him up at the airport, carrying flowers in my arms, a scarf artfully wrapped around my head to hide the lateral scar and missing strip of hair across the top of my skull, I was so nervous. And then the worst happened. He was distant. Odd. Unromantic. A week later, he broke up with me. He wanted to date other girls, he said. The pain from the breakup was searing. It felt as if I were carrying around a raw burn where my heart should be. Worst of all, I was convinced it was due to my "differentness." I was convinced that

I was not enough to keep him. Not smart enough, clever enough, sexy enough, pretty enough, "normal" enough. I was ugly. Not just ugly—*freaky* ugly. I built a prison for myself in which every possible door out led to this brick wall of an answer.

With many years of hindsight, I can see that we were simply very young and not well suited to be love partners. We would have made—and did make for many years—better friends. It's a syllogism I think about sometimes: If love conquers all, and all is timing, then why doesn't love conquer timing? But it doesn't always.

Now, if I were a less honest person, I would tell you that having a chronic illness/only one eye/being disfigured doesn't matter. I would spout that Hallmark-card bullshit about how "True beauty comes from within." But I suspect that you know this is not true, just as I discovered it is not true. The somewhat painful reality is that it does matter—*to some people*. Those particular people will not be able to see past our physicality in order to open up the awesome Cracker Jack prize inside. They will judge us on what makes us a little different and translate different as "less than." You know what? Fuck 'em. Okay. That's not very nice of me. What I meant to say was—no, seriously, fuck 'em. That is exactly what I meant to say. Move on. Just as you were smart enough to recognize the toxic nature of that girl who kept ditching you for other people, recognize that these people are not worth your time, energy, and your big, beautiful heart, dear Hoping. Theirs is a pretty limited view, and it's not your job or my job to try to make them feel comfortable about being so superficial. We are on the bus to better days, and that bus is painted in bright, rainbow colors and spattered with joy-glitter.

But there's something else at play here, too, dear Hoping. Something insidious that should be mentioned: As women, we are not taught to feel okay about ourselves just *being* ourselves. Ever gone to a drugstore and compared the women's products to the men's? Even the language is coded to make us feel bad. They use words like *correcting* and *defying* and *repairing*. As if who we are has to be fixed constantly. We receive these messages Every. Single. Day. Over a lifetime, it's corrosive. It eats away at us in ways we don't always register. Learning to dismantle this self-doubt apparatus and replace it with some self-kindness and self-love has been a lifelong journey.

Women are constantly fed the idea that we are not okay uncoupled. That we only exist or are defined by our relationships to other people, especially in regard to romance with men. I am definitely not trying to say that your desire for love and romance isn't important. It's wonderful that you want that and I want you to have that. I'm just saying that these messages exist and we do battle with them. You know what isn't talked about enough? The joys of male-female *friendships*. Which is why I'm thrilled to hear that you have this loving, close relationship with your best guy friend. Some of my most formative friendships were with awesome guys. Friendships that have endured to this day. Friendships that gave me perspective on an experience that I didn't have and that showed me what I ultimately wanted someday in a romantic relationship: love, mutual respect, laughs, honesty, openness. Somebody who would play light-saber wars in Spencer's Gifts. Somebody who would say, "You've got this. I believe in you."

As for your parents' love story, I can understand the heavy expectations that raises for you. Hey, it's wonderful that they met so young and have enjoyed so many years together. But that is *just one love story* out of eleventy-two billion love stories out there. (Those numbers are approximate, dear Hoping. I don't do math.) Some of my friends who married young are on their third marriages. They are different people now and make different choices. It's hard to fathom at nineteen how much change happens over the years, my sweet, but it does. One of my friends married the first boy who proposed to her because she thought she was supposed to say yes. That marriage made it a year. Another friend got married and we took bets on how many months their marriage would last. They just celebrated thirty years together. One of my best friends, she who was the most beautiful and sought-after of us all, the one who seemed like she would breeze through that whole love/dating/marriage thing, somehow managed to date every boy who stomped on her heart. She didn't get married until she was well into her thirties, when she found her true love at last, a man who was every bit as soulful and XL weird as she is. She is very happy.

Me? I got married at twenty-nine, long after many of my friends were coupled. I pursued my husband, not the other way around. I realized that if I wanted him to know that I liked him, maybe I should just cut out the sighing-by-the-telephone routine and call and ask him to a movie. So I did. He said no. HE. SAID. NO. Say what? (We finally ended up going on a date. I'm just saying, our love story doesn't start with hearts and roses but with comic gold.) He had no idea I liked him. None. Because he's an idiot. But this goes to show, dear Hoping, that there are worlds going on inside other people's brains, too, and sometimes, many times, actually, it has nothing to do with us, per se.

Often, those people are fighting their own internal battles. They, too, fear rejection. Or they're trying to live up to unrealistic standards of perfection. They want to impress a certain crowd and adopt everything about that crowd in order to fit in. They want to belong, too, and don't know how and they stare up at the moon alone in their rooms at night and wonder if they will ever find love. Humaning is hard. I've found over the years that my mind can rush to fill a vacuum. I can assume the worst. I'll worry that I've been too open, too honest, too messy, too much. *They all hate you*, my brain tells me at these moments. *They hate you because there's something seriously wrong with you. They are having a party RIGHT NOW and you are not invited. Because you suck.* (Sometimes, my brain is the WORST. FRIEND. EVER.) Usually, the truth is that the people I'm imagining hating me are thinking about themselves. They've got a deadline at work or they're worried about money or their skin broke out in a rash and they've been hiding away in a basement with some ointment. It's not about me at all. Learning to separate our shit from other people's shit is a skill that we develop over time as we become more conscious. Which is why I'm going to tell you one of the things that helped me the most was finding a really good therapist. In therapy, I learned the tools for figuring out what was my own stuff and what was somebody else's. I was better able to understand myself and to know what made me happy. I only know that the more I began to live my life for me, strangely, the more I began to find the sort of companionship I wanted.

This popcorn is really good. I'm glad we decided on butter.

Finally, my dear Hoping, you ask: *"Is it okay to wear your heart on your sleeve all the time or should you close yourself off? How much of yourself should you let show when meeting someone you might like the first time?"*

Oh, my sweet, this is a question that also speaks straight to my soul. I am far from nineteen, with many years behind me, but I still struggle with this question from time to time. I can only say that it is a constant negotiation. I think we get smarter about figuring out who we can be our true selves with, warts and all, and who we can't. We find our people eventually.

I'm still on the side of taking risks. If we closed ourselves off all the time, we'd miss out on so much of life's accidental wonder. Life would be painted in gray and beige. It would be like living inside an IKEA catalog. (No offense to IKEA, but, dude, it's ... pretty boring. Now I've done it. I will be pelted with lingonberries at every event.) You want what we all want: You want to know you're on the right path because you believe that if you're on the right path, everything will work out and you will not get hurt. The money-back guarantee. There is no such thing, my sweet. Pain, mistakes, failure, heart-stompingness, embarrassment, rejection, frustration, anger, loneliness, and occasionally feeling alienated are all part of the ride and are every bit as important as love, laughter, joy, excitement, success, romance, hope, accomplishment, and trust.

Often, things are much more malleable than they seem. Problems can be worked through. Hurt feelings can be discussed. Painful feelings are ephemeral and we have to hold fast to a piece of furniture and wait for them to pass through us like a violent storm. What we make peace with, my dear Hoping, is acceptance. Acceptance of our flaws. Acceptance of other people's flaws. The truth is, we are never really finished. We never really "arrive" at ourselves. We keep changing and growing. We dust ourselves off when something doesn't work. We learn to love ourselves when it feels as if no one else does (which is usually not true and is just us projecting our own feelings of loneliness onto the world at large.)

The bottom line, sugar, is that we have to be who we are. Who else can we possibly be? There is no one-size-fits-all and no amount of trying to shove ourselves into a premade Person Box is going to work out. You will burst through as yourself eventually, so it's easier and less painful to just be yourself. (Yourself sounds kind of awesome, frankly.) If you are an open-hearted person, how wonderful! Be that. But also, you will perhaps need to be selective about the people to whom you choose to give your great big, open, loving, free heart. I have learned from hard experience that if being around a person or persons makes me feel bad about myself, my gut is initiating its early-warning system. It is sounding the alarm that maybe that's somebody I need to keep at a polite arm's distance.

It's hard to expose our tiny, green inside selves to the outside world for fear that a giant's foot will come down and trample our fragile leaves reaching toward the light. We do not want to be broken. But sometimes, we will be broken. I think about unconditional love a lot. Sometimes I wonder if there is any such thing because we humans get all human-y with our resentments and pettiness. I believe there is *workable* love. I believe we can continue to grow larger on the inside, like the Tardis. I believe that life can surprise us with the sheer force of its gobstopping beauty and the tenderness of two people deciding to connect. And I believe in you, dear Hoping for a Chance.

I'm sure that if you wanted a boyfriend, any old boyfriend, you could have one tomorrow. But it sounds like you have specific wants for a boyfriend, as you should. Maybe that boy will show up tomorrow. Maybe he will show up five years from now. Maybe he won't be anything at all like what you imagined. I can't see into the Magic 8 Ball of the future and neither can you. All you can do is take a deep breath, commit to being yourself, and step into the world with that gorgeous open heart of yours.

What I'm mostly hoping, dear Hoping, is that you will give yourself a chance to love yourself first. And everybody else can get in line.

Thanks for the popcorn. And for trusting me with your question. I am so rooting for you.

P.S. Seriously, though—stay away from the ducks. Those fuckers are mean.

I was drawn to him, like a moth to a flame—only in it for the burn.

—*Blood and Salt*, Kim Liggett

Dear Heartbreak,

I was sixteen. I thought I was in love. I had this boyfriend who treated me so well and was so nice to me. I felt really lucky that someone that nice could like me. After about six months of being his girlfriend, things started going downhill. It was like once he got comfortable with me, he started to show who he really was. He would tell me who I could hang out with and tell me what I was allowed to do. He would make a mistake and make me believe that I was the one to blame. He would look at me and you could just tell that he was judging everything about me. He made me feel so bad about myself. I'm still not sure why I didn't leave him then.

After about fourteen months of being together, he started demanding sex from me. I told him firmly that I didn't want to. He didn't care. He would bug me about it every day. He always had new arguments that he would use to try to persuade me. I wanted to leave him, but I was scared. He said such awful things to me that I was scared to leave him. This bugging went on for about six months until he realized he wasn't going to get any-where with me. So instead he took me out to dinner and sexu-ally assaulted me in his truck. He called me the next day and acted like I had consented. He didn't even think what he did was wrong.

I can't even begin to describe to you what it is like to be violated like that. I trusted him with everything I had, and all I got in return was betrayal. I tried to convince myself that I was fine and nothing was wrong. I was afraid to talk to my parents or the police. I kept everything inside. One day I told a close friend of mine what had happened. He laughed and said it was my fault. He asked what I was wearing and if I acted like I wanted it. I knew things about him that no one else knew, but still he sided with my boyfriend. A month later I finally had the courage to leave my boyfriend. He wasn't okay with me leaving him. He even tried to convince me he had cancer to get me to stay. He called me over and over until finally I had to block him. That same friend from before told my ex that I had cheated on him. My ex became angry. He would contact me on every social media known to man. I had to block him on everything just to get away. He would create fake accounts just to see what I was up to. I had to delete my accounts. He called me from other people's phones and I became afraid to answer an unknown call, just in case it was him.

After he realized that didn't work, he started going through my friends to get to me. He threatened to go after my friends and even threatened to kill them because of me. Soon after he started doing that, my friends stopped talking to me. Eventually I lost them all. Before the start of my senior year I finally broke down and told my parents what had happened. My parents were extremely upset and my dad (of course) wanted to kill him (he didn't). We agreed to send me to counseling. At that point in my life I couldn't even have another person touch me without getting flashbacks. My one request was that I didn't want to press charges. I relive the assault every day and I didn't want to have to do it in front of a jury. My counselor at the time called the police on me. And again I was betrayed by someone I thought I trusted. I had to make a statement and talk to the officer that came to my house. Surprisingly, he told me that it wasn't my fault and it didn't matter what I was wearing. He said that I was not responsible for his actions, I was only responsible for my own. He was the first person (besides my parents) who told me those things. Instead of pressing charges, the officer went to my ex's house and told him to stay away from me. I haven't heard from the ex again.

A month later, I started my senior year of high school. I had a mental breakdown a few times because I just couldn't cope with what had happened to me. I couldn't believe that I had no one to confide in. No one thought I was worth being friends with. I walked to all my classes and ate lunch alone. I felt like I didn't have anyone left. I had to go to prom with girls I didn't even know. I finally got the courage to go see a counselor at school. She helped me through everything. After months of therapy I finally felt like myself again. Two years after my assault I am still friendless. I'm in college now and I'm afraid to make friends. I'm afraid to trust people because everyone I ever trusted let me down. I feel like I have no one. Will I ever be able to make friends again? Will I ever be able to trust someone again? Will I ever be able to date again?

Love,

Lonely

WE'RE NOT ALONE

Dear Lonely,

I cried when I read your letter.

I cried for you. I cried for me. I cried for all girls this has happened to.

Because we're not alone.

Sometimes when I'm walking down the street, I try to process the statistics. One out of four women has experienced sexual abuse. I try to see it in their faces, the way they move, the way they dress, but we're good at hiding things.

And I was one of the best.

I grew up in a small lake town in the Midwest during the '70s and '80s—I spent my summers in a bathing suit, running around with skinned knees and a Kool-Aid-stained grin—I'm not saying my life was perfect; I was a quirky kid. I wasn't into sports. I liked to sing and dance, which was pretty weird in my community, so I spent much of my time alone in the woods, making up stories and games to keep myself company. I was lonely, but there was an undeniable spark burning inside of me. I knew that one day I was going to use my talent to get out of there and do something spectacular with my life.

When I turned thirteen, boys started to take notice of me; I even won a beauty contest, which made the other girls hate me. I was long and lean with tanned skin and hair the color of spun sugar. I loved having the attention. It was fun—a lot better than talking to myself in the woods. I had a quick string of boyfriends, sometimes a different one every few days. It was innocent. Pushing each other off the dock. Holding hands under the water. A few kisses under a capsized sailboat.

One evening, toward the end of summer, I got invited to a bonfire/campout. This wasn't any bonfire, this was THE bonfire with all the cool kids. And I was about as far from cool as you could get. I couldn't believe my luck, and when the hottest guy came over and handed me a wine cooler, I felt like I was dreaming. I remember actually pinching myself to make sure it was real. He was three years older than me, absolutely gorgeous, an athlete, an all-around dream guy that everyone wanted to be near, and he was talking to *me*. He asked me all kinds of questions about myself. Laughed at my corny jokes. Introduced me to all his friends. Didn't pay any attention to the high school girls vying for his attention. He even wiped the chocolate from the corner of my mouth from the mess I made of my s'more. He made me feel important, cared for, like I mattered. And I kept thinking, if he sees something in me, maybe everyone else will, too. It felt monumental, like after this night, my whole life was going to change.

And I was right.

As everyone started pairing off, he asked if I wanted to go in his tent. He told me we didn't have to do anything . . . we could just talk. I remember thinking how cool and grown-up it was for him to say something like that. I knew I was supposed to go home, but I was afraid that if I left I'd never have this opportunity again. I didn't care if I got grounded. Because this would be worth it.

As I followed him inside, I was nervous, but excited-nervous. Sweaty palms, nonstop grin. With the cicadas serenading us in the dark, we lay down, side by side. There were a million stars that night and a moon so bright I could still see every detail of his face, the rise and fall of his chest with every breath. He said he couldn't believe that we'd never hung out before. That I was different from the other girls. Special. He turned on his side, twisting a strand of my hair around his finger, and told me how pretty I was, that I looked like the girl from the Velamint commercial, and then he kissed me. It wasn't the fumbling, strained, accidental-teeth-bashing kisses I was used to. This was something else. He kissed me with a hunger that I wasn't sure I liked. He put his hand down my bathing suit, touching my breasts. Or what I had of them. But his touch was too rough. Whatever he was doing, it didn't feel good; it hurt.

I finally got up the nerve to tell him I was tired, that I needed sleep. I laughed and blamed the wine cooler, that it must've gone straight to my head.

"Stay," he said as he smiled up at me, that charming smile. "You can sleep here. I just want to hold you."

And that's all I wanted, too.

So I stayed.

Turning away from him, I curled up into a tight ball. He put his arm around me. I felt the weight of it like he was trapping me there, and soon I could feel his body pressing up against mine, every part of him.

He whispered my name. I pretended like I was asleep.

But that didn't stop him.

As tears streamed down my face, he slid the bottom of my swimsuit to the side. That's the first time I left my body.

I went back to the woods, feeling the dense foliage press in all around me, and made up a story, one that would make this okay.

I waited, frozen like that, until I felt him get up and leave the tent.

It was just before dawn when I walked home with blood-stained thighs. I knew something was wrong, but I wasn't exactly sure what had happened. I blamed myself because I didn't say no. I didn't say anything at all.

And the saddest part was that somewhere in my mind I thought this meant that I had a new boyfriend. That maybe this is what it was supposed to be like.

But he never called. No one did.

A week later, long after my grounding was over, I finally found the courage to leave my room. I was walking along the lakeshore when a boy who had been at the bonfire pulled over on his bike, wagging his eyebrows at me. He told me he heard what had happened. I felt the blood drain from my face, the sharp pain pulsing between my legs. Apparently, my dream guy went around the lake telling everyone that we had sex, but that he was never going to hook up with me again, because I was a bad lay.

I remember feeling a strange heat move through my entire body, like I could catch fire at any moment. I thought it was embarrassment . . . shame, but it was something else.

I buried it at the time. I buried everything.

I did my best to repair the damage. I didn't wear my swimsuit anymore. I kept to myself, kept to the woods, but it felt like I was covered in bruises that no one else could see.

And when school started back up, things only got worse. People didn't even bother lowering their voices when they talked about me anymore. They made lewd jokes, laughed in my face, wrote vile things on my locker, pushed me in the halls.

Not only was I a slut, I was a bad slut.

And one day I got so sick of it, I decided if they were going to call me a slut, I might as well be one.

Soon, I forgot all about my plans to get out of there and do something with my life. I didn't dance. I didn't sing. I didn't care if I lived or if I died. A year passed in a drug and alcohol haze with an endless string of conquests. Nameless. Faceless. In the back of pickup trucks, fields of dried-up corn, dirty basements, against the hood of a tricked-out Mustang, where slipping in and out of my body became as easy as breathing.

It was almost like I was practicing for something, but for what?

It wasn't until the following summer that everything clicked. There was a party at the lake, and he was there. My dream guy. The guy who ruined my life. My first instinct was to run, but why should I run? I was different now, surely someone that he would want to be with. I played it so cool. We joked around, took a few shots. And when I asked him if he wanted to go on a walk, he looked surprised, maybe even a little wary, but he was clearly intrigued enough to go with me.

I found myself leading him back to the same spot where we had our first encounter. I wondered if he even remembered or if it was just another summer night to him. I started kissing him, taking off his clothes. I did all the things I was supposed to do. Everything I'd learned. And when I left my body, I didn't go back to the woods this time, I hovered above us and watched. I thought I would look powerful. After all, I was on top. I was in complete control this time, but all I could see was that little girl from the summer before, her knobby spine bulging from her skin, crying, desperately trying to fix things . . . to change her story.

When it was over he said, "You've certainly changed."

But I could see it in his eyes—he didn't mean it as a compliment—I was too dirty for him now. He liked it better when I was trembling, frozen, and meek.

The girl in front of him scared him.

She scared me, too.

When he left, I crawled to the water's edge and threw up everything inside of me. But no matter how hard I tried, I couldn't purge myself of that feeling. I'd been called every name in the book, all but one . . . *victim*. And that seemed like the dirtiest word of all.

I didn't want to feel like that anymore.

The very next day, I stopped partying. I stopped collecting boys.

People still talked—they were cruel beyond measure—but I had a plan to get out of there.

And I did.

At sixteen I became an emancipated minor and moved out on my own.

I'd like to tell you that's where my story ends, that I lived happily ever after, but it was just the beginning.

Running away didn't solve my problems. I was no longer the town slut, but it felt like those words were etched deep into my flesh. It left me vulnerable to years of inappropriate, abusive, and boundary-less relationships. I ran from one bad situation to the next. I ran from the pain, until I finally hit a brick wall. I got so depressed that I slipped out of my body and couldn't find my way back.

I spent a few months in the hospital, slowly coming back to the world. It forced me to sit still and face what had happened to me. And when the feelings returned, I felt that strange heat move through my limbs once again and I knew what to call it—*rage*.

It was the most painful time of my life, but I survived.

I still struggle with self-image, my sexuality, guilt over the choices I made; but the darkness that used to take years, months, weeks, days, to pass through me has turned into moments. Fleeting moments of darkness that I acknowledge and let go.

What happened to me when I was thirteen will always be with me, but instead of kicking that little girl when she's down, I pick her up and cradle her in my arms and tell her, *It's not your fault. You're worthy of love.*

And I'm starting to believe it.

Every time I hear a story like yours, it feels like someone's pressing down on a deep bruise. It's uncomfortable. A feeling I want to avoid at every turn, but it's okay to hurt. It's okay to cry. It's okay to feel. And most importantly, it's okay to rage against what happened to you. It was wrong and you didn't deserve it.

I don't have all the answers.

But here's how I know I'm going to be okay: I'm writing this.

Here's how I know you're going to be okay: You're reading this.

And just like that, we're connected. Sometimes that's all it takes to remember you're not alone in this world.

I believe in you.

Love,

Kim Liggett

He was different in many ways.

—*Little Elliot, Big City*, Mike Curato

Dear Heartbreak,

Being gay is hard. I love it, though. It's the most essential part of me. But with that comes the constant pressure of someone finding out. I'm out of the closet, I have been for a year and a half, but I'm still crushed into a space where I can't be myself. There are people in my classes who judge, joke, and laugh at being gay. It is my biggest fear for them to find out. It breaks my heart to have to hide, and for all the others who have to hide. Every day I craft a shell, pushing down who I am to avoid the threat of ridicule. Maybe I'm being paranoid, but I don't dare take a chance. I see these hetero boys overcompensating for their masculinity and bragging about their dicks and prowess in sports and romance, and I feel disgusted that these boys hold such (unwitting) power over me. But that is the way of society and social structure.

Maybe you can't help me. I don't know what kind of answer I'm looking for, but what I do know is that this is something that affects me every day. I sound selfish, but that can't be helped. I guess I'm just looking for the comfort that someone who is not hypermasculine or steeped in the homophobic subtext of our society is hearing this, and that others are in the same situation.

Thank you for reading.

Signed,
Boy Who Is Trapped

STAY YOU

Dear Boy Who (Thinks He) Is Trapped,

I agree, being gay is hard. And I also love being gay, despite whatever suffering I've endured because of it. Just to put you at ease, I want to share my credentials with you. I've been out of the closet for sixteen years. I am definitely not hyper-masculine. I enjoy watching a good period piece, I love going to brunch, and I happen to look stunning in heels.

I digress.

When I was in school I was not out. Buuut, it wasn't a stretch of the imagination for people to figure out that I was gay. I was clueless about sports and my voice was (and still is) effeminately high-pitched. On top of that, I knew nothing about pop culture, I was really clumsy, and I didn't know how to dress myself. My hairstyle was . . . well, I can't really use the word "style" to describe it, so we'll call it a "hair-pile." I was an easy target, low-hanging fruit (no pun intended), and I was picked on a lot. People said some pretty cruel things, and sometimes I was physically threatened, though I was never beaten up.

Let's start with a little practical advice:

Make a safety plan. Who do you trust? Where do you feel safe? If you don't have answers to these questions, don't panic. Look around. For me, the art room and library were my safe havens. I trusted my art teacher and knew I could talk to her about anything. While it's a smart idea to notice who to steer clear of, take note of who you *don't* usually pay attention to. There are other people lying low too, who are also just trying to get by without being made fun of. I made some unlikely friendships with some other "weirdos." I still talk to one of them (and I actually consulted him while writing you this letter). He was into heavy metal and dressed all in black. I was into Fiona Apple and wore a lot of plaid. He smoked cigarettes and cussed like a sailor. I was a goody-two-shoes and went to church every week. He was straight. I was . . . not necessarily saying that I was also straight. But we both liked art, and we were both preyed upon by jocks, and so that was enough for us to start talking. And though we were so different, we understood each other, and we were there for each other.

I also did a lot of stuff outside of school that made life bearable. I had a pen pal (and still do!). She and I told each other everything. Every time I put a letter in the mailbox, my worries felt a little lighter, and every time I received a letter, my heart felt a little fuller. I took art lessons at a local studio, and eventually started working there a few hours a week. I spent a lot of time at my local comic shop. I also joined a Boy Scout troop in a different school district, and met other guys who weren't exactly part of the "in-crowd." Getting outdoors on hikes once a month to breathe the fresh air was a lifesaver.

I mention this because while being gay is *an* essential part of who you are, it's not *the* essential part of who you are. We are three-dimensional beings. I excel and fail at many other things besides being gay. I'm a writer and an artist. I love watching movies. I love the outdoors and the smell of campfires. I have a sweet tooth. I enjoy reading biographies about queens (the other kind of queens). I am an awful bowler, and I am amazing at karaoke. I am a son, and a brother, and an uncle, and a friend, and a husband, and a puppy parent.

Try not to worry what people will think about a *part* of you. Show them *all* of you. Show them how good you are at being you. The people who don't feel threatened by your honesty are the people you want to hang with.

Now, you might be thinking, "That's easy for you to say, you're not in high school anymore." And you'd be right. I don't think there's anything scarier than being hated and feeling trapped, and you couldn't pay me a gajillion dollars to do it all over again. Here's the thing. Those people I used to be scared of, the people I grew to hate, I actually pity them now. I know it seems hard or unfair to ask you to have compassion for the people who are mistreating you, but being a teenager sucks for everyone. Think about how low someone's self-esteem must be if they need to belittle others to feel good about themselves.

It's a distraction to call attention away from whatever it is that they feel insecure about. Most people are in the closet about something; it's just not always that they're queer. Some of us don't fit in the closet. Some of us are a little too fabulous, so the door doesn't quite shut, and people can glimpse in and see us dancing by ourselves under a disco ball. And they will point and laugh, and we will cry. But because I went through that and survived, I am strong AF. I can emotionally bench press any one of those jocks who used to call me a faggot. Meanwhile, I bet one of those overcompensating boys you mentioned is actually gay too. And he is terrified. And you will adapt to living your life in the light much faster (as I did), while he will be fumbling in the dark for a long time, just trying to find the closet door.

It's a delicate tightrope we walk in life, a balance between feeling safe and being true to ourselves. But I can tell you that the world is so much bigger than your school. There are many people who will appreciate you being you (myself included). High school is boot camp for life. It's a really dumb pre-req that we all have to take to get to the good stuff. And you *will* get to the good stuff. And you might even have some good times along the way with your fellow weirdos.

So for now, stay strong, stay safe, and stay you.

Much love,

The hard way is my favorite way to learn.

—*All Our Pretty Songs*, Sarah McCarry

Dear Heartbreak,

Why do you like to visit oh so often? How can I avoid you? Am I at fault for seeing you so much? Maybe I am. Maybe I am the reason that my love life is completely nonexistent.

Why do we like to set our standards on love so high? Yes, every girl dreams of the perfect boyfriend. But is there really such a thing? Every time I find someone that gives me that wonderful flutter in the pit of my stomach, nothing ever happens. It makes sense, though. Why would the nice-looking, popular boys want me—a not popular, average-looking, flat board of a girl? I don't blame them. But can't a girl dream?

Why is it that I fall head over heels for any boy that glances in my direction? Or even a boy who hardly knows that I exist? This is what makes you, Heartbreak, come to visit me all the time. Am I really this desperate? I'm finding all of my friends finding boyfriends, but why can't I? How have I become a ninth wheel? Will I ever not be? I always say I don't care. My friends say that they can't see my dating anyone. And I laugh and shrug it off. But that really hits me.

How, in a school of 1,200 people, can I not find anyone? I know when boys like me, but why are they always nobody I want? What am I doing wrong? Any advice could help. It couldn't hurt to stop spending my weekends alone.

—Confusion

HOW TO FIND A BOYFRIEND IN YOUR HEART

Dear Confusion,

When I was fourteen and fifteen and sixteen and seventeen and eighteen and for a while after that I, too, longed for a boyfriend—not just any boyfriend, a Boyfriend, a fantastical chimera: part myth, part *The Secret History*, part Chris Cornell, part Miki Berenyi, part Ève Salvail, part Jack Kerouac, part Gary Oldman. The Boyfriend would be tall and lanky like me and wear clothes like mine but better; the Boyfriend would have perfectly broken-in boots and long, dark hair and eyes full of mystery; the Boyfriend would be a poet, and a musician, and write songs about me that were quite good, and gaze lovingly at me from the stage when he played them. The Boyfriend would have read *everything*. The Boyfriend would be able to quote Shakespeare at appropriate moments.

The Boyfriend wouldn't be afraid of anything, not death or long hours alone or watching your friends grow up and away from you, not the mystery of fighting through the crowds between first and second period feeling utterly unseen by the hundreds of people who passed you, not of being dumb or ugly or too big or too small or too loud or too much, too messy, too scarred-up and sad for no reason and full of broken glass and barbed wire. The Boyfriend would know my every thought before I thought it, my every wish before I wished it. The Boyfriend would take me around on his motorcycle through the rain-cooled Seattle streets, make me coffee in his apartment on Capitol Hill, kiss me until I no longer felt the chill. The Boyfriend would be at my side always, luckdragon and talisman, a charm against evil, a proof of my worth and beauty (which, of course, the Boyfriend would praise in lavish excess to all; to which, of course, the Boyfriend's own perfection would serve as wordless testament). The Boyfriend would be able to play songs on the piano after hearing them once. The Boyfriend would be older, not high school; the Boyfriend would have cheekbones like cut glass; the Boyfriend would be infinitely wise and infinitely, absolutely free. But the Boyfriend would come back to me always, my own shadow, my sustenance, my twin. Like a sibling, but psychic and way hotter and completely, totally, mine.

I remember what it feels like, Confusion, to be however old you are—fourteen, fifteen, sixteen? A little older? A little younger?—and spend all your days burning with longing for something bigger and more luminous, something like a new world or a different dimension, something like being loved. I remember feeling bewildered by what I could possibly be doing wrong, mystified by the processes by which seemingly everyone around me fell in love at the drop of a hat and professed themselves stunned by happiness. I remember all of this because it fucking *sucked*. I don't know if you will ever fall in love, Confusion, because I don't know the future, although I'd say the odds are in your favor. I don't know if the popular boys will ever look at you, or if you will get to go to the best parties, or if your Instagram will be suddenly festooned with bikini-clad snaps of you and your besties and your sun-gilt paramours lounging on beaches or boats or whatever it is popular people do for fun wherever it is you live. Where I come from they drink beer in the woods and have jet skis and it's not that glamorous. I myself was forever pining after addicts and musicians and sad old drunks who had no business whatsoever hanging around teenage girls, a course of action I do not recommend.

Anyway. It took me a long time to realize that I didn't want to be loved by the Boyfriend, I wanted to *be* the Boyfriend. *I* wanted the black leather jacket, the aloof cool, the fearlessness; I wanted the whole world to run around in; I wanted to write songs that made people fall in love with me. I wanted to be perfect and beautiful and untouchable. I wanted to know *Hamlet* by heart and at least one of the comedies. I wanted to be good at everything the first time I tried it. I wanted to be clever and wise and have long, heavy hair like a witch's; I wanted to be a little bit scary; I wanted to stomp around in big black boots and skinny jeans and look like ice and shadows, a little bit vampire, a lot rock and roll. *I* wanted the cool apartment of the Boyfriend, the nag champa burning forever in a corner, the crushed-velvet curtains (it was 1996!) and turntable; I wanted to have all the right records and have read all the right books; I wanted to be beloved and self-sufficient, stripped of all my girlish wants and sappy needs. I wanted to ride off into the sunset on my *own* goddamn motorcycle forever and ever and over again on a road paved with all the broken hearts I left in my wake.

Possibly you don't care about Shakespeare and Seattle winters and the kinds of apartments grunge-reared teenagers longed for in days of yore, or the broad back of the Boyfriend against your cheek while the rain comes down around you in sheets, laughing with your heart in your throat. I liked trouble when I was your age, liked it a lot, trouble and bad seeds; maybe your heart travels in different waters. Maybe your Boyfriend is lodged in the likeness of, as you say, the nice-looking, popular boys. Your Boyfriend smells of sea and salt and has eyes as clear as glass chips gazing forever into the middle distance like a Boyfriend in a cologne ad. Your Boyfriend is good at sports, the long muscles of his back moving gracefully under his shirts; your Boyfriend wears clothes like people on television; your Boyfriend is good with horses or on the soccer team or really fucking rich: You know your Boyfriend better than I do. You want me to tell you what's wrong with you, dear Confusion, but I'm not going to, because there's nothing wrong with you at all.

I think what you're really asking me is what kind of person do you need to be to draw the Boyfriend to you, and that's a question I can't answer, either, because if there is one thing I have learned in my increasingly long life, it's that there is nothing on this planet you can do to make another person fall in love with you. You can spend years figuring out what it is you think they want and put quite a lot of work into making yourself that person, and they will turn around and leave you for someone the absolute opposite of everything they said they were looking for, not that I know this from personal experience. You can be a cantankerous old bitch determined to spend the rest of your life a spinster and then oops meet someone who falls for you, clunk, like a stone, and uproots all your nice, tidy plans, not that I know anything about that, either. Love is not a thing you can cause to happen; it's a force with its own projects and designs. And I am telling you this, Confusion, because I wonder how much of what you want from your Boyfriend is simply what you want for yourself.

No other person can answer the question of you. I'll be honest, I don't know anybody who hasn't had to learn this lesson the hard way. It's a lot to ask of another person, that they fill an untraveled landscape in your heart where only you know how to map the way. So ask yourself this: What is it that you want other than to be loved? Who is the person you want to become? There are a million things you can do that do not require anyone to fall in love with you. You can be a botanist or a race-car driver; you can take yourself to the movies; you can write novels, learn photography, move to a big city, move to the middle of the woods. You can find friends who don't say shitty stuff to you about whether or not you can be loved. You can drink coffee in the early mornings and watch the sun come up over the mountains. You can run a marathon. You can sit around all day and eat ice cream and watch silly television shows. You can teach yourself another language or ballet dancing or music production or astrophysics or cosmetology. You can become a doctor or an English teacher or a sea-captain (I have known several; I assure you sea-captain is a real job). You can build a house. You can write bad poetry until your poetry comes out kind of decent. You can teach yourself to never be lonely alone.

And for me, that turned out to be the trick, in the end. Not to meet the person who would make me right but to find the person I had wanted to be all along. Which is not to say I've gotten there; it's just to say that after all this time I have some idea of where I'm going. I can't ride a motorcycle to save my life. I am not good at everything the first time I try it. I know some lines from *Hamlet* and a scatter of quotes from the better-known comedies. I own several pairs of perfectly broken-in black boots and stomp about in them to my satisfaction. I like being alone, a lot. I write terrible poetry and pretty good books and I never did learn to play the guitar and I am for all intents and purposes tone-deaf and I get stage fright anyway. I read *On the Road* repeatedly to impress potential Boyfriends until I realized *On the Road* is really fucking boring and doesn't have any girls in it and I wanted to drive the car myself. I did drive the car myself. I let go of trouble, mostly. I still love the rain and I still think about that apartment of my teenage dreamscape, even though I live a different life now in a different city. I cry a lot and I am terrified of the future. I am writing another book. It is not a love story.

I wish I could tell you everything will be okay, dear heart, but the truth is, all I want is for someone with authority and clairvoyance to tell *me* that everything will be okay. I can't tell you anything about what will happen next. But I can tell you that the only thing you have control over is the person you become. So put your boots on, baby girl, and go out into the world. I got your back.

Love,

P.S. It is completely, 100 percent possible to be flat as a board your whole life and still be adored. I promise.

I make the decision then, to be brave, where once I was timid. To be a different person, a better person.

—*The Black Key*, Amy Ewing

Dear Heartbreak,

Everyone has the wrong idea about you. They think you're a thing, a feeling. But I know the truth. I know it from the weeks I spent staring at the wall with dry eyes because I knew blinking would just create more tears. I know because of all the times I fantasized about holding you one last time. You're a person. A person with chocolate eyes and hair the color of night. You're arms that used to hold me together when my world was falling apart. Now I'm left all alone with my broken pieces. Desperately trying to replace your arms with my own. It's not like you didn't warn me. Even before we got together you warned me you would break me. You warned me how you would end me. I should have realized that you didn't see a future with me when we weren't even together yet and you were thinking of the end.

Words will never be able to describe the pain and the insecurity after being left. So many questions are left unanswered. For all the trouble, I wouldn't change a thing. At night when it's safe to dream, I run through all my favorite memories. The evenings we spent tangled together. It wasn't sexual—we just enjoyed being in contact and cuddling together. The times I spent in the kitchen watching you work in your element. Those were some of my favorite memories of you. When you looked happy and focused. The stress seemed to leave you and you were free to be yourself. I was never happier than when I was with you. I knew in the deepest corner of my mind that we wouldn't work. How could we? After two breakups already I knew we had issues, but I was devoted to trying to work them out with you. You didn't feel the same. After all, you are my heartbreak. I begged you to talk to me, to work this out. I didn't want you to leave me. But you did. Being friends is bullshit. It's impossible. How could I stay just friends when I'm absolutely in love with you?

My heartbreak. You don't help me any with the writing you send me. The beautiful pieces that are oddly tragic, since I know their end. They describe me in a way I've never seen myself. As magical and amazing. Awe-inducing. Rendering others speechless. They reflect my own memories from a new view. Memories of lazy afternoons with orange light streaming in and outlining you in gold. My head resting on your chest as I listened to your heart pump beneath me. The times we lay together and I felt at peace. My jagged edges were soothed and all anxiety was suddenly missing. You can't imagine the strangeness of that. Anxiety is a piece of me. A gnawing ache constantly in my soul. But you chased that away, dear Heartbreak, you made me safe. And relaxed. Relaxed enough to sleep in someone else's home. Relaxed enough to allow you to sleep in my bed. But how did it all go wrong? Why wasn't I enough for you? I'm so tired of feeling second best. Was it all fake? I know you used me as a rebound, and I'm sadly okay with it because otherwise how would I have known what it feels like to love someone enough to put their feelings and needs above your own?

Even now, I can't share anything that runs through my mind for fear of it upsetting you. My own well-being has taken a backseat to yours. I listen to you cry about your ex. How she left you. You can't see your own hypocrisy, my lovely heartbreak. You've left me. You read me your writing and it all speaks of forever and trying and loving and family. But you lied. You left me. You left me all alone. You left me and took my home. You took my happiness. This isn't fair. None of this is fair. Why do you get to leave me and then come back to unload all your issues on me? I can't handle all of this along with my own problems. There isn't ever an opportunity for me to talk to you about what I'm going through. Why does my mind always look out for your well-being even at the cost of my own, when you couldn't care less about me? It's not fair. I'm tortured with thoughts of how I'm always second best. A second choice to you.

Sometimes I believe I can't take any more. But I'm slowly healing. Slowly, so slowly. But every conversation is a stake into an open wound. Heartbreak isn't how it's portrayed. It's so much worse. It's devotion to a person who no longer wants you. It's obsession and depression. Somehow, some way, I think I'll be okay. I know I'll always love you. I'll always miss you. First loves don't go away. First heartbreaks linger even longer. But maybe one day I will be able to remember you and smile knowing what we had was something, even if it's gone.

Always,
Abandoned, 17

I AM TIRED OF TRYING TO PROVE MY WORTH

Dear Abandoned,

There's a quote from Maya Angelou that goes, *When some-one shows you who they are, believe them the first time*. It's the sort of thing that seems obvious when you think about it—if a friend always shows up late to dinner, for example, they are telling you they are a person who will be late. To expect them to arrive early would be foolish. It's the same with rela-tionships. If a partner tells you, through his actions or words or both, that he is someone who will put his needs above yours, that he will take without giving, or hold you to stan-dards he doesn't hold for himself . . . believe him.

Your heartbreak told you who he was—he said he would end you, he left you again and again. Why is it so hard for us to believe them, to pack up our bags and say, *Okay, well, you aren't the person for me, then*, instead of sticking around and hoping things will get better, that we can fix the relationship because we want it to work so badly? I promise you, Abandoned, I'm still working on this, too. I'm still ignoring it when men tell me who they are, holding out hope that they'll change, that things will be different.

I wish I could say being hurt gets easier as you get older, that you somehow develop a greater resilience to it. I wish I could say I understand what I want and what I need now, and I only choose the right people to give my heart to. I wish I could say I don't blame myself every time a relationship collapses, that I don't wonder what I did to chase him away or what I could have done to make him stay.

For years I have lived with this secret terror that I am too old to be wanted anymore. Society says I should be married and well on my way to having babies right now, and society is a master at peer pressure. No room is left to wonder if this is really what I want—to be loved by someone forever—because it has to be, because it should be. Isn't it what everyone wants? Being held in someone's arms, being kissed before bed every night, being told they are loved? But in my mad desire to attain this ideal, I lost sight of the most important love in my life: *Me*.

I want to love myself.

God, that sounds so cliché, and it is, but I'm not saying I have to love myself before I can love someone else. I'm saying I *want* to love myself. Full stop. Not in relation to loving someone else, not so I can achieve love with another person. I want to love myself with no qualifications or comparisons. I want to like hanging out with me. I don't want to twist myself into knots to try and be whoever and whatever *he* needs, to show how good I am at being a girlfriend. I am tired of trying to prove my worth.

I want to tell myself who I am. And more importantly, I want to believe it.

I recently realized that all the men I've dated who have called me selfish only did so when I wouldn't do what they wanted, when I pushed back on their opinions or demands in some way. That word—selfish—has haunted me, made me hyperaware of everything I say and do. It is my kryptonite, my poisoned apple. It is the shackles around my wrists and the gag in my mouth.

Fuck that. If being proud of myself is selfish, then I'm selfish. If enjoying my life is selfish, or sleeping until noon is selfish, or traveling to other countries is selfish, then I'll shout about my selfishness from the rooftops. Because I'm sick of living the alternative.

The first time I compromised my needs for a guy was in high school. I was eighteen and graduating and he was sixteen. We worked at the same grocery store. Let's call him Dale. He was very funny and confident and he wanted to be around me all the time. I felt overwhelmingly *needed*, and it felt good. When you said your heartbreak soothed all your jagged edges, eased your anxiety . . . oh, Abandoned, how well do I know that feeling! The sense of release that comes from needing someone and being needed is intoxicating.

We almost broke up before I went to college. And he was the

one who instigated it. It made sense. I was going to New York; he was staying in Boston. And the sheer panic I felt, of being left, of losing him, as if I would never meet another man ever again, as if he would be the only one to want me this way, to love me this way—it was a taut, burning, physical fear. It's the fear that makes us put our own well-being aside in favor of theirs, isn't it? I can track that fear's progression throughout my life and my relationships. It has a different form and grip each time, but at its core, it has the same beating, pulsing heart: *This is your only chance. No one will love you if this person doesn't.*

So I begged him to stay with me and he did. I honestly can't remember if Dale was abusive before I went to college, though I'm sure there were hints of it, and if you asked my mother she would likely respond with a resounding YES. But I do remember the day I moved into the NYU dorms—I believe it was a Friday and my parents had driven me down with all my stuff and helped me put sheets on my bed and unpack my clothes and set up my desk. And we went out to lunch and I just lost it. I had to go home, I insisted. I wanted to see Dale, and he wanted me to come home—he had been the one to suggest I come back for the weekend, even when I had only just arrived in the city.

My mother wanted me to stay, but my father said I could come home, and so I lost my first weekend alone in New York. I came home and saw Dale and the tightness in my chest eased. He was happy I was there with him and I was happy he was happy. I went back on Sunday and the stress and fear returned.

It became a requirement that I had to talk to Dale every night before bed. If I didn't, he would yell that I was cheating on him. I remember vividly one night when I woke him up to say goodnight and he was so tired we just decided to talk the next day. Come morning, he was furious with me for not calling him, and no matter how many times I insisted that I did, *I promise, babe, I swear I love you, I called, I promise* . . . he didn't believe me.

I started coming home on weekends and not telling my parents. I stayed with a family friend who had been a mentor to me during high school. I spent the money I had earned over the summer on bus fare. I did it for him, to prove to him that he was the only one, that I loved him. But it was never enough. He constantly berated me and put me down, calling me a slut and a whore. He was paranoid and jealous, sometimes to a scary degree. I can still clearly recall the day I was in his kitchen and we were making lunch and he turned to me and said, "Even if you came home every weekend, I would still think you were cheating on me."

He said this to my face. He told me who he was—a guy who would never trust me no matter what I did, no matter how much I worked to prove my faithfulness.

And still, I stayed. Because who was I without him?

I barely went out at all my first semester. But as hard as Dale tried, he couldn't prevent me from making friends. And two of my closest friends happened to be guys. We were all in the same acting studio together and they were wonderful and fun and always talking about the cool bars or restaurants they'd go to, plays they would see, concerts they would attend. Things I couldn't do myself because if I didn't call Dale at a very specific time, he would lose his mind and I would suffer for it.

I can't quite remember what the last straw was, but I do know that when I came home at Christmas, something felt stuck inside me. I had spent a semester making new friends and watching them grow, seeing them go out and get to know the incredible city that is New York, turning from high school kids to college students. I felt like a puppy on a leash watching from a window. And deep down, in a place I had been ignoring for months, I knew the reason for my isolation. I called my mother at work and said, "Mom, I'm not sure if I want to be with Dale anymore." And my mother—who absolutely *hated* this boy, and for good reason—took a breath to control her own feelings on the matter and said, "Well, what does your heart tell you?" She knew if she said, "Dump that asshole immediately," I would have balked. That's just the way I am—stubborn to a fault.

"I don't know what my heart is telling me," I wailed. But that was a lie—I did know. My heart was shouting at me, screaming so clearly now that I was finally allowing myself to hear it. And so I called Dale over to my house and ended it that day. He cried, and I cried, but in the end I felt so much better. Free. Light. And I had the most incredible second semester in New York.

He sent me an email at the beginning of my sophomore year, just checking in and hoping I was doing well—of course, most of the email was dedicated to what *he* was doing, successes he was having, where he was applying to school. I decided to write him back. I thanked him for reaching out and said I was happy he was doing well. Then I proceeded to inform him—with examples—of how his behavior had been abusive and manipulative and cruel. I tried to be diplomatic, but I'm sure I didn't entirely succeed.

His response was chilling. The friendly banter of the previous email was gone, replaced by a harsh, grasping, angry boy who couldn't acknowledge what I had to say. One line in particular has stuck with me: "I didn't make you feel like a whore; the things *you did* made you feel like a whore."

But I was stronger now. And I didn't believe what he said about me anymore. He had told me who he was and I saw him now: a controlling, bitter person who needed to put me down to make himself feel better.

I wish I could say that my relationship with Dale was the only lesson I needed in matters of the heart. But life doesn't work that way. This heartbreak will likely not be the last you suffer, Abandoned, however much I truly wish it could be. And there are no words of wisdom that can fully prepare you for the heartbreaks still to come, no letters or quotes or proverbs that will magically give you the power to make only the Right Choices. Wrong choices are a part of life—you know this. You're already looking ahead to the day your heartbreak won't be such a brutal memory, when you can look back on this relationship and remember the good times without the pain. I was so impressed by that sentiment, Abandoned. And that, I *can* promise, will happen.

But I want to share with you the pattern that I fell into, in the hopes that you might be able to recognize your own someday, or avoid having one altogether. And I want you to know you aren't alone.

I acquiesced—I think that's the best way to describe my attitude in relationships. I gave in. I decided that my feelings weren't as important as theirs. I truly and sincerely did not know who I was without a boyfriend. It gave me a sense of security, like a photo in a wallet I could take out and say, "See? My life has meaning." I was part of The Couples Club and the thought of losing membership was terrifying.

Which was probably why I stayed with Alan for so long.

He was ambitious and successful, the kind of person that was always planning exciting trips for long weekends, or going to concerts, or eating at nice restaurants. I thought he was so much better than me. He had his life together. I was a struggling graduate student. He had a gorgeous apartment in Tribeca and I moved in because it made sense; we were always together anyway.

Alan wasn't a bad person. And I believe he truly loved me. But he was the one making the decisions and I was expected to follow along. And I did. He promised he would stay in New

York but when a better job offer came, he abruptly left me for Johannesburg, expecting that I would go with him, uprooting the life I'd built for myself here. I stayed when he told me we could survive long distance and I moved to Joburg for an entire summer to be with him. I stayed cooped up alone in a house all day, with no friends of my own, waiting for him to come home and be with me. I was the puppy on the leash again. I stayed with him when he told me he got a job in New York again and it was only a matter of waiting for his visa to come through. I stayed and waited and waited and stayed.

But he had told me who he was too: He was in charge, he was the boss. We weren't a team or an equal partnership. So I shouldn't have been surprised when he said he wasn't taking the New York job. He expected me to keep waiting until he'd found exactly what *he* needed. And why shouldn't he? Hadn't I been telling him who *I* was, every time I said *all right*, every time he made a decision without taking my thoughts or feelings into consideration? I told him I was a pushover, that my needs were secondary, and he believed it because it was exactly what he wanted to hear.

I finally gave him an ultimatum, but instead of having the hard conversation and facing up to the fact that this relationship was ending, the man I had spent the last three years with simply vanished. No phone call, no email, nothing. Just gone. I saw a picture on Facebook a couple of months later—him and a new girlfriend, all smiles with his nieces and nephew. And it hit me that he had been waiting for *me* to end it. I saw him in an entirely new light, no longer the ambitious successful man with the sort of life I aspired to, but as a boy who put himself first and took the easy road. It is easy to disappear, to avoid the messiness that comes with a breakup. And it is acutely painful to the person left wondering what happened, where she went wrong, how it got to this.

I think that's what led me to Baruch. He was the opposite of Alan in every way—dark and brooding and incredibly sexual. He made me feel desired in a way I realized I never had before. He was a drug to me. And like a drug, he came with highs and lows. Baruch never worried about having the difficult conversations. I think he enjoyed telling me he couldn't see me anymore, only to come back into my life a week later. You know what I'm talking about, don't you, Abandoned? It hurts worse when they come back, even when it feels so acutely, deliciously good at the time.

Throughout that entire week we were apart, I would be devastated. The pain of him leaving was worse than with Dale, worse than with Alan. It was a chain around my ankle, pulling me underwater. It was an ache in my stomach that nothing could soothe. I needed him so fiercely I threw everything I was away—I never talked about myself and he didn't want to know me. He wanted the me *he* wanted, little snippets here and there, taking only enough to satiate his needs. He was an addiction I didn't want to kick. And I honestly don't know if I would have been able to if he hadn't moved to Miami after two years of exquisite torture. Physical distance was the only rehab that worked.

He told me he would never be my boyfriend. And he never was. But if he had stayed in New York, I would have kept holding out hope that if I just gave him more time, eventually he would see how we should be together. Even as my heart, so hoarse from screaming the truth at me, cried, *No no no. He isn't right for you.* I was so much more concerned about trying to make sure *I* was right for *him.*

I tell these stories proudly now, because they are a part of me. They have shaped the woman I have become and led me to the place I am in now. Slowly, ever so slowly, I am starting to love myself. I am starting to worry less about getting old, about being undesirable, about never meeting anyone who will like me ever again. I am trying not to put everything into whatever man I might have one remotely successful date with. I am starting to ask myself, *Is this what I want?* instead of *Am I what he wants?* I am beginning to break a pattern I thought was unbreakable.

I am not fully forged yet—my metal is still glowing red-hot, being shaped and molded, but I know what sort of sword I want to be now. You are still in the fires, Abandoned, still malleable. Who knows what sort of sword you will become? You have time to craft yourself, to forge your own shape. And you will be stronger than you thought you could be.

As for me, I have told myself who I am. And I'm ready to believe it.

Love,

I'm sorry, but I don't get it. If we're supposed to ignore everything that's wrong with our lives, then I can't see how we'll ever make things right.

—*Please Ignore Vera Dietz*, A.S. King

Dear Heartbreak,
Fuck you.

Sincerely,
Done With You

WHO SAID I HAVE TO GIVE MY HEART UP FOR BREAKING?

Dear Done With You,

Oh, I get it. I really get it. Let it all out until all that's left is a big, fat Fuck You. Fuck you, heartbreak. Fuck you, love. Fuck you, people. Fuck you, world. Fuck all of it and all of its relatives and any sheets it ever slept in.

I have been there, Done With You.

I have been there.

But let me stop and really try to figure out what your letter means. It's only two words long. It's clearly full of emotion—anger and probably frustration, if I was to guess. And sadness. And maybe loneliness as well. And let's face, it—it's a lack of patience. Because who has patience for heartbreak? Not me. Not you. And so we arrive at these two words. Fuck You.

I'm with you, Done With You. I am flipping off heartbreak right next to you because I've had my share. Most recently, I've survived a twenty-five-year-long marriage that was harmful to everyone involved in it—even my kids. To which you must think: *Hold on . . . why is this woman even giving advice?* Yeah. I get it. But listen. Twenty-five years of marriage is a feat that you probably don't quite get yet. I'm a warrior. I'm a goddamned national treasure for trying so hard to make it work for so long all by myself.

Except I'm not.

I'm just another empathetic, caring human who was taken for a ride by a manipulating, scared, unaware person. This happens ALL THE TIME. And it always leads to heartbreak. Always. No matter how confident a codependent person is (which is what I was), it eventually catches up with us. The penny drops. We see that we do everything. We see we're the only ones who talk, who reach out, who hug and love, who seem remotely interested in the relationship surviving.

So now you're wondering how I got into this spot. I'm a pretty together person. I have my life in order. I do my job and then pick up another job and then another. I can make a chicken dinner last all week in many forms spanning many types of cuisine. I can do push-ups. I know when to back away from bad friends. I know when to say no. I don't drink to excess; I don't do drugs. I can juggle two basketballs and an apple while taking bites of the apple. I can handle just about anything you throw at me. And I'm proud of that.

But the one thing that has happened to me over and over again is: Men walk all over me. (Or women. I've been walked over by both.)

Let's deconstruct. Let's go back in time. Let's look at my ingredients and see how this cake got made.

You have a kid who never felt loved all that much. That's me. A kid who's never been taught the value or meaning of self-love. Also me. A kid who loves doing things and doing them well. Me again. And you let her loose in a culture obsessed with coupling. She gets walked over time and time again. What else did you think would happen?

I needed love, I needed to feel good about myself, and I needed everything to be perfect. No failure allowed. That's how I got here, Done With You. By being too damn strong for my own good. But most of all by being quite naturally needy. Because human beings need things and there's nothing wrong with that. Except sometimes there is.

Life can be cruel, right? I got used to being made fun of early on—always with my short hair and my boy's clothing and my shop class and my other "weird" quirks. I didn't think I was weird, but others did. And little by little, people learned that when they made fun of me, I'd take the high road because it's what I do. But it doesn't mean I wasn't hurting on the high road. I was. I've had crazy things said about me and those things ate away at my self-esteem in a huge way. Even if they were stupid.

(One time in college, a bunch of girls passed around a rumor that I liked to have sex with goats. That was 1988. It took me until 2015 to realize that I wouldn't have known where to find a damn goat if I wanted to. Now? I can find you a goat. Name your day. I can find you a damn goat. But at eighteen, I didn't know where to find a goat. And yet for nearly thirty years, that rumor really bothered me. As did many others. They made me feel small. Made me feel less loved than I already did. But it took thirty years until I realized HOW STUPID THAT SHIT WAS. Goats? Really? They couldn't come up with anything more realistic than goats?)

So we're used to the hazing ritual that is childhood by the time we get to be teenagers. And then the hazing gets worse. Adults join in (if they weren't already there) and we land in a shit sandwich. Our own peers are still telling us how unworthy/ weird/unlikable/into goats we are, maybe our families, too, or teachers, and then we get to be teenagers and the entire world hates us. Let's be really clear here—this is not in your imagination. A majority of adult society completely disrespects teenagers. Toddlers are damn cute—even when they make mistakes. Add ten years and you're suddenly an asshole for every mistake you make. The eye-rolling is audible. The sheer exhaustion teenagers seem to cause adults is ridiculous. And they think your heartbreak is stupid.

Seriously. Hey, adults: YOU ALREADY LIVED THIS SHIT. How come you don't remember how hard it is?

Maybe we block it out. In fact, I'm pretty sure we do. I remember having my heart broken when I was a teenager. But I don't remember the pain. It's a bit like childbirth, I guess. Our brains forget. We say dumb things to our teenagers. Here's one I've said recently to my teenager: "Why don't you just try to do this year only thinking about school and not date anyone?"

Yeah. I've said that. And I meant it. But I forget how this is nearly impossible. In our teens, we are forming ourselves. We are exploring the world. We are exploring other people. And we fall in love. Even if we're not ready. What's ready, anyway? Seriously. Who is really ready for love? None of us.

So do me a favor and think on where your self-esteem sits right now. Check yourself out. Take a weekend to write down all the things you like and don't like about yourself. And then figure out which things are in the wrong columns. Example: I used to think that being smart (as a girl) was a thing I didn't like about myself. That's some bullshit, right? But that idea was formed by the boys who'd say mean stuff to me because I was smart. And look at me now. I make money off the shit I make up in my smart brain.

So, ingredient number one: self-esteem. Do you have it? Has it been whittled down by years of social interaction with callous peers? Figure this out. It won't just help you with heartbreak, it'll help you with everything else in life. And it will probably lead you to the next thing I'm going to talk about.

Heartbreak will be on the menu if you didn't have love in your life growing up. I'm just going to put this out there. If you had a childhood that was weak on love (no matter how new your sneakers were, no matter how much food you did or didn't have in the fridge—it's not the stuff, it's the LOVE), then you're going to have some heartbreak if you don't get some things straight first.

Find a way to love yourself. Don't argue with me on this because it sounds like I'm a weirdo cosmic hippie. You need to be okay with you before someone else is. Their love for you can't stand in for your own. Period.

This relates to: Choose, when you can, to be happy ALL BY YOURSELF. Because if you're thinking someone else can make you happy, you're in for a long, painful ride.

I'm not dishing this out of superiority. This is real. It's important. More important than algebra and your Spanish homework. You have to realize that the world has it wrong. Our culture doesn't really ever talk about this stuff. And yet it's the most important stuff you could ever learn. So hear me out. Yes, Fuck you, heartbreak, but hey, since I'm already sitting down at the bottom of a well of sadness, I should probably look around and figure out what the hell got me here because it wasn't the fault of just one person. (Not even me.)

It's time to get healthy.

Have you had some bad shit happen to you? I mean as a kid? As a teenager? Look at it. Figure out how it's affecting you NOW. Because if you don't, it will affect you forever. Trust me on this. The sooner you can start sifting through the dirt at the bottom of your well, the sooner you will be able to be happy all by yourself, and then eventually be happy with another person.

Ingredient number two: expectations. So, about those two words you wrote to me—the anger and frustration they express—I need to ask you a question. Have you ever heard of the friend zone? Are you aware that it's a myth that's used to blame others for anger and frustration in love? Let me explain.

The friend zone by definition is really the disappointment

another person feels when their own (often unrealistic) expectations are not met. It's a way of manipulating you into thinking that their expectations are your responsibility. Read that again. *It's a way of manipulating you into thinking that their expectations are your responsibility.* That's what it is. The friend zone didn't exist when I was in school. I am grateful, because I was a smart girl who took shop and most of my friends were guys and yeah, some of them fell for me but usually I was too busy hating myself to notice. But holy hell, at least those guys didn't have some messed-up idea that because I was breathing, or dancing next to them, or sneaking out for a cigarette with them, I was supposed to be their *girlfriend*. That's nuts. Like—psycho nuts. To put it simply: Just because someone wants to be with you doesn't mean you have to be with them. You haven't put them into a zone. They put themselves there. And if you feel as if you've been put into a "zone" by another person, it's time to have a good look at where your expectations came from and ask yourself if you're being fair. Are we clear? Good.

While we're on the subject, I want to talk about loneliness. Loneliness is a human experience and everyone has it. Coupling up with someone doesn't cure it. I like to look at that feeling—at its desperate worst—and see something good in it. Because if I don't find something good in it, I end up pointing my finger outward. And that's not cool, Done With You. If I'm lonely, it's my job to figure out how to be alone and happy and not blame someone else for making me feel lonely. See also: the myth of the friend zone. Blaming others for our loneliness is really an expectation problem. Sadly, no one tells you in life that you will be lonely. I'm glad I can be the one to say it if you haven't already heard it. Loneliness is a human experience. It's normal. In relationships and not in relationships. Ride it out like you ride out a head cold. It'll get better.

And I should add this, because it's super important: No one should yell at you, make you feel small, make you do things you don't want to do, or make you feel like shit for being yourself and doing whatever you want to do. Ever. As humans, we lose it sometimes and that's okay. But unless there's a heartfelt apology and understanding conversation after experiencing another person's anger, it's time for you to really think about what you're doing and why you're doing it.

To summarize: Anger, frustration, and loneliness are all going to come at you during times of love and heartbreak. Make sure that you regulate your expectations of other people and of yourself. Stay emotionally healthy. Stay away from people who aren't.

Ingredient number three: Bake your own damn cake. My sister has a friend who, during a time in her own heartbreak, said to her, "Who is chasing you?" which is a quote from an old movie. This isn't meant to sound creepy. It's a legit question. If you're chasing (i.e., showing attention to) people you're romantically interested in but they aren't chasing back, there's a good chance you're looking for someone to complete you, and there is no such thing.

None of us is born half-finished. We are born whole. You need to be whole before you love another person. We all have gaps inside of us. Love gaps. And no one can really fill those gaps for you. That's not anyone's job but yours. Worse yet, if you find someone who wants to make you happy all the time, then you've found someone who is probably filling their own gaps with you— not with themselves . . . and that's going to be a problem. We are not puzzle pieces looking around for our match. We are whole people looking for other whole people with whom we'd like to spend time.

Here's where our education has it wrong. No one talks to us about being truly healthy. Oh, sure, here's the food pyramid and some advice about exercise and maybe a little half-assed, unbal-anced, hetero Sex Ed if you're lucky, but no one talks about dependency and codependency and how chasing other people might mean we're desperate for love we never got when we were kids. They roll their eyes and call drama if teenagers dare look into themselves. Do you want to know why? Because, like me, many adults are living lives of heartbreak and pain while pre-tending we have our shit together.

No one has their shit totally together. Ever. Anyone who says they do is lying.

But the closer we get to knowing what healthy means, and to being healthy ourselves, the less susceptible we'll be to heart-break. We don't pick the people who are trying too hard to impress us. We don't keep a partner if they've tried to hurt us or make us doubt ourselves. Healthy people don't do that. And yeah, it hurts when we realize that a person isn't who we thought they were, but if we're healthy about staying healthy, then we know what's truly best for us.

I have to be honest. If there was one thing I could change about my years in high school and college, it would be to take away this pressure to be WITH someone before we ever are encouraged to be WITH ourselves. I wish our bodies could turn off that urge to mate until about age twenty-five. God, that would be nice, right? I mean, the culture does it to us before the urge even hits. I got married to some kid named Mike in third grade on the kickball field. I know kids who were fake-married as young as kindergarten. And y'all, that's bullshit.

How, in a culture that forces us to think about coupling so young, do we ever form ourselves fully? I don't know. But I do know that it's the key to happiness and the key to healthiness.

I'm so done with heartbreak, too, Done With You. I'm done with feeling empty and unworthy and jaded. But I'm also done with the IDEA of heartbreak. Who ever said I had to give my heart up for breaking? Who ever said that this was supposed to start so young? Who made these rules? And why the hell are we following them?

I am happiest when I'm alone in my office writing books. Or alone in a hotel room after a day speaking to an audience. Or alone on an airplane flying to a new country. I am happier alone as long as I'm healthy. And because I'm happy at all those times, I'm happier than happy when I come home to my family.

As for my husband of twenty-five years? He got help. He realized what crazy shit was in the bottom of his well. He's labeling it and processing it and figuring it out. He's getting healthy. At fifty years old.

Don't wait that long to look around at the bottom of your well.

Please, Done With You, if you haven't already, seek a healthy life. You were born whole. Make sure you're intact before you think about love again. And don't worry—if it feels cold and impossible for now, that's normal. If you need love, then give it to yourself. Learn how to say no for your own good. Stop believing the myth that we are born to be coupled. We aren't. We are born to kick the world's ass all by ourselves. Companionship is a bonus, but only if it doesn't break your heart in the process.

Heartbreak can go fuck itself. But let it go. Let the pain go. Let the people go. Let the whole thing move into its rightful place in your past. Free yourself. I can already tell you're the kind of person who doesn't take shit from heartbreak. So don't take any shit from anywhere else, either. When people give you shit, leave it on the side of the road; don't pack it for the journey.

While the world told us that we were supposed to be Disney princes and princesses, they were lying to us. Maybe the moviemakers thought a single character couldn't be a love story. But we can be. All by ourselves. Love stories.

Now go dance to your favorite song while wearing your favorite clothes and make your favorite food, okay? Because nothing says *fuck you* to heartbreak more than that. Nothing.

Love,

Amy ♡

I think with some people you can just tell you're
going to have a history with them. Even if that history
hasn't happened yet.

—*Here We Are Now*, Jasmine Warga

Dear Heartbreak,

I'm dating a boy who is poisonous. In many ways we are similar. We both like the same things, we both play sports, we both have the same sense of honor, we both care about each other. I know he loves me, and I'm not sure if I'm in love with him yet, but I know I love him. When we first started dating, my best friend had feelings for him, which I was unaware of. I'd constantly ask her if she did, and she would never tell me, so I figured I had the go-ahead. I realized after a month of unspoken words and weird unknown distance, I was wrong. We tried to talk about the situation, which for me made it worse. She told me that she loved him, and from here I didn't know what to do.

He had feelings for me, he picked me, and he made me feel loved. I didn't want to give up something that made me feel happy and made me feel loved, cared for. I was stuck. I knew if I broke up with him, he'd be devastated and I'd be hurt, and overall, what would that do for my friend? It wouldn't mean she could date him, but maybe it wouldn't hurt as much to see that her best friend was no longer with the boy she loved. So what do I do? Do I sacrifice my own, his, happiness so she would not be hurt? That doesn't seem fair. It doesn't seem fair that all this time she'd say nothing about her feelings until it was too late. Until she realized what she had lost.

But what about me? *I love him.* He loves me. I don't want to lose him. I want him. Like a drug, addictive, yet poisonous. I don't want to hurt her; however, I am happy and don't want to hurt myself or him. Either way, someone gets hurt, and it sucks. I don't think there is a right or wrong answer. It's simply him or her? Either way, I lose someone I didn't want to lose. Either way, I sacrifice. Either way, I was put in a situation that is unfair, that is challenging, that is hurtful to someone.

—Undecided Girl

OWN YOUR HEART

Dear Undecided Girl,

My junior year of high school, my best friend S and I had a crush on the same boy. Though *crush* is probably the wrong word—we watched A as he floated down the halls. He was a year older than us. He was a mystery that we wanted to solve.

My and S's friendship was centered on things we both liked. We both liked to read pretentious books that we thought our other classmates probably couldn't understand, and even if they could, they wouldn't *get it* like we did. We both liked the same obscure (or at least obscure to us) indie records. Especially the angry-girl ballads. We both wanted to be seen as manic pixie dream girls, but knew enough not to say that aloud because then you automatically were not one. We both wore clothes from Urban Outfitters and Anthropologie, but lied and said we found them at thrift stores.

But as silly as all of that was, I also felt truly bonded to S. She was someone with whom I could be completely honest about my fear of going away to college. My worries and insecurities about everything from my physical appearance to my intellect. We crafted our carefully curated personas together, but it was only with each other we were able to let go of those personas.

And as I said, we both were fascinated by A, and so it felt like a miracle when at the end of senior year, my path crossed with A's and he showed interest in me. The first night he instant-messaged me (a reference that is sure to give away my age), my heart jumped into my throat just like all the angsty indie rock songs I'd been listening to had said it would.

With S, I detailed and analyzed my every interaction with A. She would come over to my house and help me craft messages back to him. When I'd get home from going out with him, I would call her and relay in excruciating detail every single thing that happened. I knew in the back of my head that S had also once been interested in A, but her crush on him didn't seem like a big deal. We never talked about it. Not once.

And it wasn't a big deal until I went away to school. Right before I moved away to college, A and I broke up. Though "broke up" is probably the wrong word because we both considered our-selves too bohemian to label our relationship, but we had been together. And when I left for school, our arrangement dissolved. I was not happy about this. Being with A had made me feel cool. Confident in a way I hadn't before. I was upset, but pretended I wasn't.

When I got to college, I was lonely. I was homesick. I pre-tended I wasn't. I was a student at the fancy school I had been dreaming about going to for years, but I was lonely. I missed my

Midwestern hometown. I missed its provincialness that just weeks before I'd been desperate to escape.

Two weeks into being away, I got a call from S. She was now sleeping with A. I totally lost my shit. I couldn't believe that she could hurt me like this. Didn't she know about girl code? I moped for days and days, secure in my place atop the moral high ground. I felt crushed and replaced. And lonely. My god, I felt so lonely.

I felt totally victimized by S. I told myself that I would never do something like that to someone I cared about. But yes, darling Undecided Girl, you are right—I already had. I had been rather careless with S's feelings when I constantly flaunted my relationship with A in front of her. I had been cruel when I hadn't even bothered to talk with her about her feelings. I had brushed them off—acted as though ignoring them would make them disappear. And if the situation had been flipped, I knew in my heart of hearts that I would be doing exactly what S had done.

But I still tried to make S pay for the pain she had caused me. I told her that I wouldn't be her friend if she kept seeing A. And guess what she did? She kept on seeing A. My ultimatum accomplished exactly nothing except for me losing my friend.

You are probably trying to find the thread here, Undecided Girl. You might be wondering what my reckless and damaged eighteen-year-old heart has to do with your precious undecided one. But my dear girl, it has a great deal to do with you. Because from reading your letter, I've decided that your biggest problem is not figuring out what you want, but learning to accept and own what you want. You don't have an undecided heart. You have a heart that you have not taken ownership of.

What I am trying to show you by laying bare a lot of my adolescent drama is that people hurt other people. We even sometimes hurt people we care about. When you are young, you have a wild heart. The boy you are dating also has a wild heart and so does your friend. Wild hearts want what they want.

Your situation, darling, is quite simple when you boil it down: You and your friend like the same boy. You have been blessed with the extraordinary good fortune that the boy you like likes you. That is the only difference right now between you and your friend. I am sure that she has convinced herself that if she were you, she would step aside. She would choose your friendship over the boy.

But I am not sure that is true. Actually, I am almost positive that it isn't true. Remember: Wild hearts want what they want. This is why I get so mad when people rant about "unlikable" characters in novels. Everyone is the unlikable narrator of their own story. We all want things we shouldn't. We all want things that sometimes hurt other people. Even people we care deeply about.

Policing someone's heart does not solve the problem. You cannot make someone who does not love you, love you. You cannot make someone not love someone they love. When I was your age, I used to listen to "All My Little Words" by The Magnetic Fields all the time. On that track, Stephin Merrit wisely sings, "And I could make you rue the day/But I could never make you stay." And this, *this*, my darling girl, is exactly what I am trying to impart to you. You can never change the will of someone's heart. You can punish them. You can threaten them. You may even be able to convince them to try to act against its interest, but you can never change how their heart actually feels.

Once you accept this truth, life may seem a tiny bit less painful. You have created a false dichotomy for yourself. You do not have to choose between this boy and your friend. This is not a choice between romance and friendship. You only have to let your friend understand that you care about her, but you also like this boy. Those two emotions are not as incompatible as you believe. You have to let her know there is room in your life for both of them. She may be mad, but ultimately she has more of a choice to make than you do.

She can either dig deep and decide to let her love for you trump her own disappointment that the object of her affection does not return her feelings, or she can wallow in that disappointment. I hope she will not choose the latter. There is nothing for her there in that well of disappointment and her bitterness will only eat her alive from the inside. I know—I have been there.

One of the most difficult things I have ever had to learn is how to hold space for two conflicting emotions—to learn how to be happy for a friend when they are given something that I wanted. My most basic instinct in these upsetting situations is to resent my friend for having the good fortune that I didn't. But I have now learned how to clamp down on that feeling, to lean hard into my love for my friends, to let my love for them be greater than my own disappointment. To understand that they did not take whatever it was that I wanted from me; to understand that the thing I didn't get was simply not meant for me and that is a fact regardless of what has happened to my friend. To understand that holding that kind of toxic jealousy inside of me is a slow death and if I let my jealousy kill me, I will not be around to have other triumphs.

You are going to have to ask your friend to love you more than she resents you for having what she wanted. Again, this is her choice to make. Not yours. When it was my turn to make this choice, when I was in the position of your friend, I chose wrongly. I hope your friend does not let you down in the way that I let S down. But I do think that if you engage your friend in an open dialogue about the situation, you will be much more likely to end up with the outcome you desire. Both S and I were doomed by our own respective inabilities to articulate our feelings. Maybe we were both scared of them; I don't know. But I do know we didn't own them and that was our biggest problem. We let our secrets and our silence run like a river through the foundation of our friendship, eventually cracking it into pieces.

A part of you probably expected that I would answer your letter by preaching about girl code. We, as women, are often taught by societal messaging that to be a good friend is to sacrifice our own happiness. We are taught to shrink our desires, to make ourselves smaller so that other people can be more comfortable. Fuck that. As you state, even if you break up with this boy, it will not erase your friend's heartbreak. It does not solve her problem that the object of her affection does not return her feelings. It only serves to make two more people upset. This is not a reasonable solution. It, in fact, is not a solution at all. Because—think about it—even if you acquiesce and end your relationship for the sake of your friend, will that really solve the problem? There is a chance that your hurt over ending the relationship will fester into a deep wound of resentment that will cause major problems in your friendship.

I'm the mother of two tiny (and absolutely adorable, thank you very much) ladies, and I want to raise them to be kind. To be good friends and good people. Capital-G Good. I want them to care about others, about the planet. But I do not want them to think that to be nice is synonymous with sacrifice and suffering. That is a lie that has been sold to us female folk by the patriarchy for far too long. In this particular situation, you can be a good friend by being honest and by being empathetic. You can tell her you are sorry that your relationship brings her pain, but ending your relationship would cause you pain. Her pain is not worth more than yours; your pain is not worth more than hers. This is not a situation where there is nobility in sacrifice. There will be times in your life when that is the case, but this is not one of them. Do not be tricked into thinking otherwise.

Sweet girl, you need to understand that life is not something that just happens to you. You, darling, make life happen. Own that. There will never be a point in your life when you won't inflict bruises, but part of growing up, part of doing the real work of becoming a responsible human being, is learning to own those bruises. You must be honest with your friend. You must tell her that you love this boy and you are sorry that your love for him causes her pain, but you must—you must—own your love of him. You need to let her know exactly how important this boy and your relationship with him are to you.

Laying this truth bare for your friend—owning this love you have for a boy who loves you back—will require courage, but it is much more noble than waltzing around the issue, pretending as though you are an actress simply reading the lines you have been given. Pretending that you are some sort of victim that has been put into an impossible situation. Undecided Girl, you are not a victim.

Life is not a play. You were not cast as the star by sheer good luck. You write the script. And the script you are writing involves you dating a boy that your friend also likes. This is messy, but it is survivable. As I have now said a dozen times, I think your friend's pain will be lessened a lot (I mean, A LOT) if you take ownership of your feelings for this boy. If you truly lean into them and let your friend understand the depth of your love for both her and this boy.

Before we end, I want to address one little thing that has been nagging at me. You begin your letter by declaring, "I am in love with a poisonous boy." This made me flinch. When I think of a poisonous boy, I think of a boy who is cruel. Who is abusive, verbally or physically. Who is a mean snake who needs to be kicked to the curb, smashed under the heel of your boot.

However, the rest of your letter does not leave me with the impression that this is actually the case. But if it is, run for the hills. Run as far as you can, sweet girl. Leave this boy behind. If he is actually harmful, you need to tell someone. I implore you to do this. There are too many men in this world that believe they can abuse women. Do not let him get away with his cruelty. You deserve so much better.

As I said, though, from your letter, I have not been given the impression that he is harmful. If anything, he seems quite nice. A boy who has managed to win not only your affection, but also the affection of your friend. Am I right in thinking that that's what you feel is poisonous about him?

If the answer to that question is yes, than I believe what you meant to say is that you are in a poisonous situation, a lose-lose predicament. But as we've already laid out, you are not actually in a lose-lose predicament, my darling. Remember, it's up to your friend to decide if your friendship will be lost over this boy. That's *her* predicament—not yours. You just have to fess up to your own feelings and be kind.

When I got so angry at S for dating A, it wasn't even really about A. It was about the fact I felt like S had never been completely honest with me about how she felt about A. Our problem was that we never talked about our true feelings to each other. It was also about the fact that my ego was bruised because A wanted S now. I felt like she was winning at something I was losing at. I hope you and your friend rise above this and do not get sucked into our society's twisted obsession with convincing women to compete against each other for the attention and affection of men. You and your friend are not in competition with each other. The boy has not chosen to like you instead of your friend—do not see your relationship as a contest that you have won. Love, my darling girl, is not a blood sport.

Let your friend know you love this boy and that you love her, too. Show her your love for her by having the courage to be honest with her. Stop slinking around your feelings. Stop pretending like this is a situation that simply happened to you. This is the bravest and kindest thing you can do for your friend. This is the bravest and kindest thing you can do for yourself.

Let your heart want what it wants. Stop pretending. Own your heart, Undecided Girl. It is yours. Own the fuck out of it.

Rooting for you,

Jasmine Warga

The truth was, maybe they'd come to the end of their path together. Maybe it was time to say good-bye.

—*When Dimple Met Rishi*, Sandhya Menon

Dear Heartbreak,

I just really don't like you. It's nothing personal, but all that you have done to other people and me is just too much.

I never really experienced you until the time I got into middle school. It's kinda hard being a teenager as it is. And having you show up does not help. It was sixth grade; I was the shy, good girl who rarely spoke. I had my little group of friends, but I preferred being away from all drama. While other girls spent hours arguing over what guy they liked and who liked who back, I spent my time writing my feelings in my journal. This was all while I developed my first crush. It was a new and exciting feeling, but I couldn't tell anyone about it because I am religious, and that kind of stuff at my age is just not tolerable. So I kept it in for years.

I continued holding my secret until I could no longer. It was the end-of-the-year eighth-grade dance, and I needed to tell him. I looked over at the dance floor. My eyes only seemed to focus on him, and I just wanted to let it go and finally tell someone. A slow song came on, and, to my surprise, he came up to me and asked me to dance. I was shocked and petrified. I only nodded my head. As we danced, we talked about our day, and he started to tell me about how "great" I did at the track meet before the dance. This was the perfect chance to tell him how I felt about him.

I took a deep breath and told him. His facial expression started to change as I finished my confession. The song was coming to an end. He looked at me and said, "Oh, I didn't know that. But I just don't think that it's possible—we're better off just friends." And with that, he walked away. With each step he took, my heart shattered.

Heartbreak, why are you so hurtful? I started to regret telling him, and started to lose my confidence. I felt betrayed, for some reason. I just wanted to make this feeling go away. It felt horrible to not tell anyone about this as well. I am Muslim. I started to think that this was the reason that he rejected me, and my heart broke even more. Everything that made me *me*—I didn't want anymore. I just wanted to be like all the other girls. But, honestly, Heartbreak, you need to stop!

Love,

Anonymous

BIGGER THAN HEARTBREAK

Dear Anonymous,

There is so much in this letter that speaks to my heart. Introverted girl who spends time writing in her journal? Check. Not allowed to talk about boys/crushes at home because of religion and culture? Check. Wondering if the boy rejected you because you're Muslim? Teary check (only in my case, it was because I was Hindu/Indian/brown/had a "funny" name).

Oh, it's so unfair, isn't it? I mean, like having crushes on boys isn't difficult enough. Add in things like an introverted personality and a culture/religion that only a small number of people in the country share and you've turned the whole love thing into a pit full of crocodiles and fire.

But you know what? In your letter, I see someone extremely kind and thoughtful. For instance, in your very second line, you say, "all that you've done *to other people* and me is just too much." Even in expressing your intense dislike of heartbreak, you're still putting other people before you. You're still thinking of them.

Here are a few more examples that cue me in to your personality and the kind of person you are: "I preferred being away from all the drama." "I spent my time writing my feelings in my journal." "I am religious, and that kind of stuff at my age is just not tolerable. So I kept it in for years."

Know what I hear?

I really care about others.

I respect what my parents and religion want from me and will put that before my needs.

I'm thoughtful and creative.

I get what you're saying, Anonymous. I feel all my feelings in the solitude of my own room, even now, as a bona fide adult. I prefer to keep away from chaos and confusion; I write my thoughts and feelings in a journal. This also means, of course, that I'm an observer.

See, I think most people fall into one of two categories: observers or participators. Participators tend to be louder, more dramatic. They tell people how they feel and they're open about what they want and what they're thinking.

We observers, though, tend to be quieter. Oftentimes, we're creative, shy, unsure. We tend to question ourselves. We're empathetic and kind, and we feel our feelings deeply. We also tend to get hurt by other people more.

It sucks being an observer sometimes. To be one is to question yourself constantly. You're evaluating yourself way more than you'll ever evaluate anyone else, because you spend so much time quietly thinking about things: what you went through, what he said, what you said, what everyone really meant. You worry what others think of you. You never feel quite enough. You feel different, other, and maybe a little bit like rejection is in the cards forever.

I don't know what makes people observers. Maybe it's some childhood experience we go through. Maybe our parents are stricter. Maybe it's genetic. But I do know that to be an observer is to open yourself up to hurt. We're softer, more willing to reach out to people. And to reach out to people is to (sometimes) be hurt. It's just the way we are. But in case all of this sounds really sucky, here's a side note: All my favorite people are observers. I find them to be the most genuine—and oftentimes compassionate—people I've had the privilege of knowing. And all of them have stories of heartbreak. Here's one of mine.

This one time in high school, I had the biggest crush on the best student in my speech and debate class. When he spoke, people stopped to listen, period. He had this really rich, authoritative voice, and whenever I had to debate anything with him, I would get all shaky (partly because I know he was about to totally kick my butt in the debate, but partly because he was just so cute).

We never hung out or anything—observer here, remember?— but I did always smile at him and say hi. So you can imagine how I felt when I was riding the bus home one day and he asked if he could sit by me. Obviously I told him yes, while sliding over and holding my legs really stiffly so my thighs wouldn't touch him (but also totally hoping the bus would go flying over a speed bump and throw me on top of him).

We talked about speech assignments and some other stuff and then I got it in my head that this was my Big Chance. Like, we hardly ever spoke to each other. But he'd asked to sit by me. That meant something, right? If he wasn't going to take the first step, I totally should just do it. I told him how I really loved his style in speech and debate (no kidding) and how impressive he was onstage. And then I told him I really liked him.

He was quiet for a long time. And then?

He *laughed.*

"You're not exactly . . . my type," he said finally. "Sorry." And then he went to sit with his friends in the back. After he'd been there a few minutes, *they* all laughed, too. I knew they were laughing at me. It sucked. Majorly.

Over the next few days I kept obsessing about his words. He'd kind of paused before saying the words *my type.* I felt sure there was a message in that. Was it obvious I wasn't his type? Well, what *was* his type? I thought back to his last two girlfriends. Both had been white, blond, and tall. I was brown, black-haired, and short. Was that what he meant? Or was it a personality thing? Why couldn't I just be outgoing and gregarious, the kind of bubbly girl pegged to be the "sexy, girl-next-door" type? Why couldn't I be like all the other girls?

I was so embarrassed, Anonymous. Embarrassed to have put myself out there. Embarrassed to have been shot down. Embarrassed to have been laughed at. Embarrassed I'd failed to see that I wasn't his type. Maybe, I thought, I wasn't *any-body's* type. Maybe I was meant to be alone. Maybe I'd live in a tiny shack with heartbreak as my pet, snarling on its leash, forever.

Like you, I couldn't come home and tell my mom about it. I knew what she'd say if I did: *You shouldn't have told a boy you liked him at your age. You're too young for crushes. This is what happens when you focus on boys instead of your studies.* Etcetera. So I held it all inside. I walked through school feeling like people were staring at me, sure that Speech Guy had told everyone, and everyone was laughing behind their hands at me. My friends didn't say anything, but maybe they were just being nice. And I was too scared to ask if they'd heard. In speech class, I sat like I had a neck brace on: staring straight ahead at the teacher and nothing else. No *one* else. Speech Guy pretended like I didn't exist, which simultaneously was a relief and broke my heart even more.

Somehow, time passed. As I got more distance from that horrible moment, I realized something: When I put my time and effort into things outside of me, things I really loved and was passionate about, it was easier to be with those parts of myself I wanted to leave behind. I hated the shy, introverted, nerdy girl I was. I hated being an immigrant and speaking with an accent. I hated that my name was, for most people, difficult to pronounce. But when I was doing something I truly loved, something I was truly passionate about, all of those things receded into the background. When I wrote a poem, my being an immigrant gave me a different view on things that people seemed to appreciate. When I was on the phone with someone in crisis at the suicide hotline, they didn't care that it was hard to pronounce my name.

So I dove in headfirst. I did things that helped me accept those prickly parts of myself that didn't fit quite right: I was a teen crisis counselor, I worked with people with developmental disabilities, I was part of a cleanup crew at the local beach, I volunteered with animal shelters and libraries, and I wrote and drew until my pencils were tiny little stubs and the people at Staples learned my name. I gave of myself whenever I had the opportunity, and every time I did that, I found myself becoming just a little bit stronger. I realized that I may not have been Speech Guy's type, but I was my *own* type. Even if I had to end up alone (spoiler alert: I didn't), I would develop my identity as a kind person.

I figured out that it had always been inside of me, that kernel of wanting to reach out and soothe others. Speech Guy had done me a favor, in the end: He'd helped bring it to the surface. And now I had something no amount of heartbreak could take away: the knowledge that the world was a better place because of me.

I see in you, Anonymous, a huge capacity for kindness. I'm sad that some guy at a dance hurt you. But I want you to know something: You *are* like the other girls. You're just as smart, just as beautiful, just as talented and kind and amazing. Maybe you haven't found that out yet. But keep searching for the thing that will help you step outside of yourself and see all the things you're capable of. I'm one hundred percent certain you'll find that you are your own type, too. You have the power within you to overcome the heartbreak from Dance Guy, to discover what you really want from this life. You contain multitudes, to paraphrase Whitman.

You're so much bigger than heartbreak.

Love,

Sandhya Menon

I wanted to smile for her, I really did. But my body was too busy trying to stop my heart from cracking in two.

—*Saving Maddie*, Varian Johnson

Dear Heartbreak,

I don't really know how to start this letter, so I'll just jump in. I am going to tell you the story of why I feel like I deserve to be lonely. For a long time, boys didn't recognize me because I don't wear makeup or short skirts. So I was surprised when my crush started to write me. I was nervous and didn't want to make a mistake. He goes to my school and is in my class, so I've known him for two years. In school we barely talked at first, because I am a rather quiet girl and in school he is quiet, too. We started to connect and got closer. We talked more in school and I fell in love. He is the first and—even now—the only boy who has shown an interest in me.

As you can imagine, I was really happy. In my school it's normal to go on a language trip to another country, a country I'd always wanted to visit. We went there in June and stayed with host families. His was close to mine and we met every day. A friend of mine, who stayed with the same family as me, was always with us. She tried to set us up and give us as much privacy as possible. This was all totally new for me. Usually I am bad at showing emotions, so it actually was hard. I have trust issues. After seven days we moved to a youth hostel. There, we had more time. On our first day I went to his room and we cuddled in his bed. Then he kissed me. It was my first kiss and it made me absolutely happy. The feeling . . . I still have to smile when I think about it. We talked a lot and made out. I really thought he would ask me to be his girlfriend soon. Of course that didn't happen. Looking back, I don't even know why I thought I would have luck. His ex-girlfriend, who's also in our school, was on the trip, too. The next day she came into my room while he and I were watching a movie and he hid. I felt so bad, because I thought that he still had feelings for her. I was too insecure to ask him about it, and he left soon after her.

Later, he texted me to come over, because we needed to talk. I was afraid; nevertheless, I wanted to make this work. He told me that his parents would never allow him to have a relationship with a girl who believes in a different religion, and that he's sorry. Sorry to hurt me. He told me that he was in love with me and he gave me a heart-shaped stone. I should have ended it, but I was naive and thought it could work. So I said I didn't care if we couldn't be together officially; I just wanted to spend time with him. We had an amazing time on the trip, but after we got back it was different. We only hung out twice after coming back. At first, we still texted a lot, but he was always busy. I started to feel like I was annoying him and like he didn't want to see me. Maybe you know the feeling, but it is one of the worst in the world. Our conversations felt cold and meaningless. During our school holidays, he was out of the country for two weeks, to visit family. He didn't even text me once. I texted him, but he didn't answer, so I stopped.

The feeling was terrible, because he posted pictures on Instagram and on Snapchat. I knew he could easily text me, but nothing came. I waited. I searched for excuses for why he couldn't write me. It was hard to accept that he just stopped liking me or lied from the beginning. I didn't want to accept it, so I waited for a message after he came back. He came back, and still no message. I never asked why. I still thought I did something wrong, but I was too insecure to ask.

After the summer break ended and we saw each other again, he said nothing. He ignored me, not one word. Not even a look—he treated me like I was invisible. I felt terrible, but who should I have talked to? I have friends, but they have their own problems, and mine are not important—at least I always thought that. So I stayed silent, too. I am the go-to person for a lot of my friends if they have relationship problems, but they never asked what happened. I feel lonely and unworthy of being loved. Now he's started a relationship with another girl from my class—you can guess how I am feeling. I am still too insecure to ask him why he just threw me away. I want to hate him, but I can't. I still care and want him to be happy. So I keep silent. It hurts to see him with her. It hurts that all my friends are in relationships and I am alone. They tell me how much they love their boyfriends and how amazing they are. Not once has someone asked how I am feeling. I feel worthless and lonely. Still, I don't say anything to them because I am afraid. I am afraid to lose them. I am afraid of them leaving me like he did. I am afraid that they will laugh about me, because they think my problems are unnecessary or ridiculous and, finally, I am afraid of being alone forever.

Love,

E., 18

LIFE IN THE FRIEND ZONE

Dear E.,

First of all, let's get the most important thing out of the way: You are most certainly worthy of being loved. I believe every human being is afforded this right. We deserve love—platonic, familial, and romantic love. And more importantly, we deserve a type of love that respects us, keeps us well, and keeps us safe.

Part of me wants to spend the rest of this letter explaining how you are better off without that jerk and how you should move on with your life. Actually, part of me wants to end it here: Get over that jerk and move on with your life!

But I've also been in your shoes—the person on the losing end of a burgeoning relationship. It's so easy to feel lonely, unwanted, and unworthy of love. It's hard to navigate relationships as a teenager. Hell, it's not so easy as an adult, either.

Another part of me wants to sit you down, hand you a triple scoop of chocolate ice cream, and say, "Don't worry. It will get better." You will graduate from high school, and go on to university or work or other experiences, and you will find someone special who appreciates everything about you. You will find ways to be less lonely, either with friends, or in a romantic relationship, or even by yourself. You will thrive, and people will see the beautiful person you really are.

But I didn't want to hear any bullshit like that when I was a teenager. All I wanted was the person I loved to love me back (which, of course, is still valid even today).

Plus, I don't like ice cream.

So all I can say now, as someone well past eighteen, is that I had a situation similar to yours—and if I can make it out okay, you can, too.

I was a lot like you in high school. Girls never noticed me—at least not in the way I wanted them to notice me. I always thought I was weird looking—super skinny, with huge clown feet and toothpick-thin legs (no lie—I was so self-conscious about my legs that I hardly wore shorts). My ears were so big that they belonged in their own zip code. I played baritone and trumpet in the marching band, served on the student council, and was a member of the chess club. I collected comic books and geeked out over all things *Star Trek*. I was one hundred percent nerd. Being a nerd is all in vogue now, but that wasn't the case in the late eighties and early nineties. We were not the cool kids. We were the kids who ate lunch while huddled in the corner, trying to be invisible.

I was also extremely lonely. I used to think—if only Tanya or Betty or Roxanne would like me, then everything would be different. Everyone will see how important I am! And maybe

I'll actually get to kiss someone for real. Or, hell, maybe I'll even get to make out! Woot!

Newsflash: Tanya, Betty, and Roxanne never noticed me. And even if they had, they were in no way interested in helping me practice my tongue-hockey skills.

Of course, movies and television shows didn't offer realistic romantic expectations. You could pick just about any cheesy high school romantic comedy and see where the beautiful girl—after pining for some superficial hunk for most of the movie—eventually came to her senses and found solace in the arms of her geeky friend—usually after said geek got his ass kicked after trying to defend his lady-friend's honor. (I'm looking at you, Daniel LaRusso from *The Karate Kid*.)

Another newsflash: I took karate when I was a teenager. That crane-technique shit does not work in a real fight. Trust me. I have the scars to prove it.

So, anyway, I spent my first year of high school fumbling through the like/lust/heartbreak cycle that I attached to any available girl, whether she was in my league or not. Then, during summer band practice, I met someone new . . . let's call her Michelle.

Michelle was trying out for the band. She was short—her head landed just below my shoulder. She had light-brown skin and small brown eyes. Her hair was in a ponytail, except for one long lock hanging down to her cheek. The tress was curled tight like a spring—I remember wanting to grab it and give it a tug to see if it would bounce. I also remember being surprised by the tenor of her voice. It was deep. Almost sultry. It totally went against the stereotype of her small, dainty frame.

It was love at first sight.

Correction. It was *one-sided* love at first sight. I was already planning what we'd be wearing to prom for the next two years. How much her parents would love me once they met me and realized how awesome I was. How we'd keep our relationship going while we went off to our separate colleges.

We quickly—and, dare I say, effortlessly—struck up a friendship. And . . . that's where it stayed for a long time. We were both so damn shy. We didn't know how to navigate romantic feelings. I had no idea how to turn a friendship into a relationship. Neither did she. But other boys did. Cooler, hipper, taller, non-geeky boys. Boys that were everything I wasn't.

As she began to revel in this attention from these other guys, I decided I'd just be her friend. That'll be okay, I told myself. Because, like in the movies, the girl always eventually ends up with the friend, and they all live happily ever after. (At least until there's a sequel—I'm looking at you, *The Karate Kid Part II*.)

And that almost happened. She did pick a friend . . . but not me. Instead, she started dating one of my best friends, another band geek. Talk about brutal. There they are, being all lovey-dovey, and I'm the fool sitting on the sidelines, hoping she'll one day snap out of it and pick me.

Their relationship didn't last long (it turned out that my friend was gay, though I don't know if he really knew it at the time). I remember when he broke up with her. He did it at school—before the first bell. Michelle's friends took her to the bathroom because she was crying so much. When he told me what had happened, I didn't know whether to punch him or hug him. I hated that he had hurt my friend, but now was my chance! Since my friend was the dumper, and had already moved on to another relationship, I figured he'd be totally fine with me trying to pursue Michelle. And he was.

But *she* wasn't. She still loved him, even though he was now with someone else.

I told myself that it was okay; I'd stand by her and be the friend she needed. I emphatically stated that our rock-solid friendship was more important than these silly, fleeting high-school romances. Which was true. It was also total bullshit. I was not-so-secretly hoping, waiting, praying, assuming that it was only a matter of time before she got over her ex. Only a matter of time before she would wisely realize that I was "the one."

And then the football player came along.

He was a bad boy with a good heart. We shared a science class together—I liked him. He was funny and charming. He knew Michelle and I were friends, so he asked me for advice about how to approach her. Being the gullible fool I was, I actually gave him good advice. But honestly, I was also a bit cocky. I wasn't worried about him. Michelle was going to be *my* girlfriend. It was destined.

I'm sure you can guess how this ended. Long story short,

they became a couple. And they seemed pretty happy. I finally got the hint and started dating other people as well—I even made out with a few girls! But none of my relationships ever lasted. These other girls were nice, but they weren't Michelle. As long as I loved her, I couldn't love anyone else.

What was worse, we would still talk every day at school, and on the phone at night at least three times a week, and she would continually thank me for being such a good friend. I kept my feelings to myself because I was trying to be that good friend she could talk to about anything. Not just good friends—by the time I graduated, she was my best friend. I couldn't imagine going more than a few days without talking to her.

It was a tough, shitty situation to be in. Every time she looked at him and laughed, my heart ached because it wasn't me she was fawning over. Every time she placed her hand on his, or he put his arms around her waist and hugged her, I felt all the sorrow and loneliness bubbling up inside, pushing against me like churning water against a dam. But I shoved all those feelings way back down, because she was my best friend, and I was supposed to be happy for her.

I thought things would be better once I went away for college. And they were, at least a little. I dated more (and made out more). I became more confident. I began to understand what I really wanted. *Who* I really wanted. And I became determined not to let anyone—including her boyfriend—stand in my way.

I crafted the entire speech in my head—what I would

say, how I would say it, even when I would take all these melodramatic pauses between words. I couldn't have the conversation face to face—I was away for the summer, and would have been too scared to talk to her in person anyway. So I played the most romantic music I could find as background noise and gave her a call.

She could tell something was different in my voice as soon as I started talking. I laid it all out—explaining how long I'd felt this way about her, and all the reasons why we were perfect for each other. I told her she was the one person I looked to for comfort when things were wrong in my life—and I challenged her to deny that she didn't see me in the same way. And she *couldn't* deny it. I *was* the person she turned to when everything was going to shit in her world. She couldn't imagine living without me. She truly loved me.

But only as a friend.

I was devastated. This was not how it was supposed to happen. I had become a better person. More confident. I was no longer the geeky band kid with braces and the weird comic book collection. I was finally somebody important and interesting I was worthy of not only being her friend, but of being her boyfriend as well.

Of course, it didn't matter to her how much I had changed. Or maybe she didn't see this new me. In her mind, I was the nice, sweet, and kind friend I had always been. But only a friend. That was that.

Looking back, I've realized a few things since then. First, it was silly for me to wrap up all my hopes for love and companionship in this one person. Don't get me wrong—as shitty as I felt during that conversation, when she told me she was staying with her boyfriend instead of choosing me, she was still a great person and it was unfair for me to put her on a pedestal like that. It wasn't healthy, and, thinking back on some of our long, late-night talks, it probably wasn't very comfortable for her. I also wish I'd been more honest with her at the beginning. No one likes painful conversations, but it's like ripping off an adhesive bandage stuck to a scab—you yank the bandage off; it's painful for a little while, and then it's over. Instead, I slowly peeled away that adhesive, millimeter by millimeter, over the course of *years*. Prolonging the conversation didn't alleviate the pain. It only dragged it out.

I wish I'd respected myself more. All I saw were the negatives about me. My appearance. My activities. But now that I look back, I can see how fucking awesome I was. I was a geek—a geek that graduated as co-valedictorian of his class. I was a nerd, but I could drop silly pop culture facts just as easily as I could quote *Star Trek II: The Wrath of Khan*. I was a jokester. I had a wealth of friends.

If I had just opened my eyes, I would have discovered that I wasn't lonely at all. I had friends and bandmates. I had all the love I needed right there.

I was perfect in my own skin. I just didn't realize it.

By the way, Michelle and I remained very good friends—once the sting of rejection wore off. A few years after my huge declaration of love, she finally approached me about a relationship. We talked underneath the stars on a cool July night. She was just as beautiful then as she'd been when I'd met her nearly eight years before. We talked, and we hugged . . . and after clearing the air, we bid each other goodbye.

Michelle was a wonderful, beautiful, magnificent person. And I still loved her . . . *but only as a friend*. I had grown and changed over the years, and had found the person I was destined to be with. So I returned home and kissed my girlfriend. A few years later, she became my wife.

And don't feel too badly for Michelle—she did okay, too. She got married, and now all four of us are good friends.

So hang in there, E.! And don't forget, you're awesome just like you are. Don't let anyone let you feel otherwise!

Love and hugs,

And on days like that I felt so fucking lucky just to have someone to feel that way about, just to feel that way at all, it didn't even matter if you felt the same way.

—*Althea & Oliver*, Cristina Moracho

Dear Heartbreak,

He was my first love. A love that we didn't know existed until it actually happened. We met in my freshman year of high school in a small school play. I thought he was fun to talk to, and I decided to send him a message on Facebook. He replied and we became really close, talking about everything and nothing. For the first time in my miserable life, I finally felt happy. We told each other our sob stories and it became evident we were both messed up and the same. I began to care for him. More than I had ever cared for anyone. He was nice and kind and sarcastic, with a great sense of humor. He was stupidly smart and sensitive and he was my best friend. During the summer going into sophomore year, I began to develop romantic feelings toward him, which I shoved down deep into a locked box in my heart. I didn't want to ruin the friendship we had. So I ignored those scary feelings and continued on with my life.

During that year, we hung out more and more, going to his house and "platonically cuddling." We were blind toward each other and we both ignored our feelings. But I didn't care. I loved the feeling of his arms wrapped securely around me, feeling his body heat warm my back, the feel of his soft breath against my neck. No matter how hard I tried, however, my feelings couldn't be hushed. He asked me out on October 30, 2015, in his car while I was taking a nap before a football game. When he asked, I was still in that weird sleep stage where I had no idea what was going on. I asked him to repeat and I'm pretty sure I said no at first. Then I comprehended what he asked and I was ecstatic. It was finally happening. I was going on a date with my best friend. The relationship lasted for one year, two months, and nineteen days. I was happy. I could hold his hand, kiss him, and know that he was all mine. That his black hair was mine to play with and touch. I knew that his brown-black eyes were only looking at me. That his witty remarks and his teasing were his way of telling me he loved me. And the way he kissed me, as if we were going to die the next day. All of him was mine.

And I loved him. He made me feel a whole different kind of beautiful in my depressed and anxious state of mind. He knew what to say to make me calm down and he constantly reassured me. He never lost patience when I was up all night asking him why he was with me, because all I wanted to do was die. He slowly started to raise my self-confidence and I began to actually like the way I looked. I began to lose the suicidal thoughts, and he was with me through it all. But all the while, I wasn't able to listen to him. He always pushed off talking about himself no matter how much I asked, and I was worried. He needed as much help as me, but he wouldn't let me save him. I'm still sorry about that.

Then it was summer going into junior year. He made a club baseball team and was out of town a lot for games and practice. He didn't have a lot of time to talk to me, and I fully understood him. Yeah, I was sad, but I wasn't some psycho girlfriend demanding every second to be with him. So whenever he was in town, we'd see a movie and we'd spend the day together. Then he was off again, winning games and sneaking late-night calls to me in his hotel bathroom so his teammates wouldn't hear. But since he wasn't there to talk, my depression hit hard and I felt suicidal again. I felt ugly again and believed that I wasn't deserving of my boyfriend. He was perfect and the boy every girl was looking for, but I was a disgusting monster who was selfish. Eventually I wrote letters and decided I would take more than enough sleeping pills to end it. I almost did. I had texted him before I started and when I was on the fourth pill he texted back with "hey, beautiful, sorry I wasn't able to talk today, are you okay?" And I cried. He was too good for me.

I never told him about what happened that night because I knew it would break his heart. So I kept that secret, and junior year started. Everything was great the first few months— we were happy and finally together. But it wouldn't last. He eventually stopped replying and started to ditch me for his friends. Now, I was perfectly fine with him hanging out with his friends, but when he never spent time with me, it started to hurt. I would frequently call him out, and he'd always apologize and try to fix it. He got better for a bit, then he went back to ignoring me. I thought it was my fault and I cried all the time, my heart breaking. We spent a day out on the town for our one-year anniversary and he was happy and I felt like he was going to try and be better. We both would. So we walked through the town, hand in hand, and I had never been happier.

That changed two months later when he broke up with me a week before Christmas. I was shocked because we both wanted to spend the rest of our lives together, but I guess I was too naive. He said he still cared about me. I think that's what hurt the most. Over the next few weeks we talked awkwardly around each other. He told me to stop texting him to try and work out emotions. I did, but I was still madly in love with him—but I didn't say so. He told me he had kissed a girl during those weeks. I wanted to cry. Those lips weren't mine anymore. Those dark eyes that sparkled weren't mine. And then he said he didn't want to be friends anymore. I hated it, but let it happen. A couple weeks later he messaged me saying that we could talk again. It was great to finally talk to him again. Then he stopped replying again and I asked to go for a drive with him. He agreed and he came over and picked me up. We talked for hours and he gave me this really sad look and said he wasn't okay. I asked him what he needed and he just said a hug. So I hugged him and he'd slowly start getting closer to my face until we shared the same breath and then his mouth was on mine and I forgot my name.

He was an asshole for doing that. For leading me on. And he left without talking about what happened. We didn't get back together. I was fed up and asked him what was up. And the truth came out. He couldn't stand me anymore. The way I acted, which he used to love, now repulsed him. He hated my mannerisms and everything about me. And he told me to stop texting him so he wouldn't hurt my feelings. Then I said goodbye and I let go. I let go because I love him. I feel empty now. He took a piece of me with him and I will never get it back. I miss him. I don't even want a romantic relationship anymore. I miss my best friend. The best friend I could tell everything to. And the worst part is that he probably doesn't miss me. And I don't know how to feel about it.

—Fireheart, Falling Apart, 17

DOWN THE RABBIT HOLE
AND OUT THE OTHER SIDE

Dear Fireheart,

   I think it would be irresponsible of me to jump right into
your broken heart without first addressing something else you
mention in your letter, something far more serious—suicide.
There was a time when you crossed the line between abstractly
wishing you could simply close your eyes and immediately, pain-
lessly, cease to exist to almost following through on a plan
involving a lot of pills and some very grim intentions. It's dis-
turbing to think about what would have happened if you hadn't
received that text from your now-ex-boyfriend while you were
downing those pills. Despite his unwitting intervention, it's fair
to say that depression this severe lies far beyond the purview
of the average teenage boy, who in all likelihood is not yet
equipped to do his own laundry, much less be your emotional
Sherpa, your personal mountaineering guide, carrying your
baggage up and down the mountain while trying to keep you
from slipping on the ice and tumbling right off the edge. In
moments of crisis you're better off reaching out to a suicide

hotline, such as the National Suicide Prevention Lifeline at 1-800-273-8255, but to properly fight depression for the long haul, you'll need to talk to a doctor and come up with a plan involving therapy or medication or both. And for that, you'll need to talk to your parents, however potentially unpleasant that may be. Only you can decide how much you need to tell them—do you want them to know just how close you came to a suicide attempt?—and while you understandably may not want to upset them or freak them out more than necessary, they do need to grasp the urgency of the situation, that this is not something that can wait a month or two, and, perhaps more importantly, it is not something they can fix themselves. Depending on their experience with and knowledge of depression, they might need a little help when it comes to understanding that there is rarely a single, tidy reason for a sadness as deep as yours, and a quick fix is unlikely.

Of course, not everybody's parents can be approached with a problem like this—maybe they're not good at hearing the hard stuff or maybe they think depression is something you can just shake off with a little grit and determination. When I first told my parents I was struggling with depression, I knew they didn't get it because they kept wanting to know *why*, as if it could be traced back to a single event, like a bad grade or a falling-out with a friend. To be sad for no reason was simple self-indulgence; what I needed was to stop feeling sorry for myself. So telling your parents might not be the answer, but perhaps there's someone else—a good friend's mom or dad with whom you have a close relationship, or a compassionate teacher whose interest in her students seems sincere and genuine. But talk to *someone*. Some things are just bigger than us, and we can't fix them on our own.

Depression does respond to treatment, though; it won't always feel like this. It will get better, and as it does you'll learn ways to keep it at bay. You'll figure out what triggers a bad episode—maybe sleep deprivation, alcohol, or a lack of structure sets you off—and teach yourself to avoid those triggers. You'll build a solid support system and learn how to make self-care a priority and your days will not always be ruled by the presence of this black cloud. And the next time you fall in love, depression won't feel like the third person in the relationship. I have been on both sides of it: I've watched helplessly as someone I cared about withdrew further and further into his own unhappiness, rejecting treatment and pushing me away, and I've been the person crying hysterically in the middle of the night unable to articulate *why*. Neither relationship lasted.

Falling in love can be easy. When the person you are in love with reveals that they love you back, it's the closest thing to a genuine miracle some of us will ever experience. And when that feeling is taken away, and you have to get by without it, it just seems like an impossible task. It's like going from a world filled with color to one cast solely in black and white. You can't imagine a time when you won't feel this way; you're convinced you will feel this way forever, unless he comes back to you.

Losing your boyfriend is hard enough; losing your best friend is devastating. Especially when you and your best friend had one of those impassioned, all-consuming friendships that was basically one sloppy kiss away from being a relationship anyway. There's something about those super-intense friendships that blur the line between being best friends and being a couple, with all that sexual tension simmering just below the surface and the greedy, giddy sense of ownership because this person is mine mine mine—these "friendships" are like rabbit holes you tumble down and get lost in for ages, and you wander around in the dark with no idea how to climb back out. They have so much appeal because they offer a lot of the benefits of a committed romantic relationship without taking scary risks like, say, telling another person how you feel about them. You get to be part of a twosome, to have the inside jokes and the secret language, to know exactly who to call when you're having a bad day. You have a person who is your person—and you get to be in love. And being in love can feel good, even when it feels bad. Even when you're not sure it's reciprocated. A best-friendship can be almost indistinguishable from a romantic relationship; sometimes it seems like the only real difference is the lack of physical intimacy. Of course, throw in some "platonic" cuddling and even that line gets blurred; it's not that you and your bestie aren't hooking up, it's that you aren't hooking up *yet*. The pain of not having this person completely is mitigated by the anticipation that one day you might because everything is pointing in that direction, and all you need to do is be patient and let the relationship evolve naturally. Right? Right. Further and further down the rabbit hole we go.

These friendships are not always quite the bargain they seem. This person gets your time, your attention, your emotional support—not to mention the cuddles—without having to sack up and declare themselves or let you off the hook by telling you they're not interested in you that way. They get to monopolize your heart without making any kind of commitment. This falls firmly in the territory of leading you on, whether they realize they're doing it or not. Some boys may be genuinely oblivious to how their actions affect you, but others just don't give a shit. I didn't want to believe that my best friend could be so callous about my feelings, so I made up a million excuses for him. He was confused, he wasn't ready, he was afraid of ruining our friendship, he was intimidated by how intense our relationship would be if he could just let go and let himself love me. For two years I pretended to be satisfied with our "friendship" while simultaneously waiting for him to come around and accept as the truth what I had known all along—that we belonged together. I missed out on other romances that might have actually been healthy, with people who knew what they wanted—me—because I was too preoccupied with picking myself apart, trying to identify which flaw of mine was holding him back.

So the next time you find yourself teetering on the edge of that rabbit hole, ask yourself whether you're willing to surrender your emotional sanity to a boy who either (a) has no idea what he wants, but is perfectly happy to keep you on the hook indefinitely while he figures it out; (b) does know that he doesn't want you, but is perfectly happy to bask in your adoration and cop a few feels during cuddle time while he waits for somebody better to come along; or (c) does want to be with you but lacks the ability to communicate basic emotions like a normal person. I know it's easy to talk a big game about holding out for someone who truly deserves you, but love makes beggars of us all. We eagerly await the tiniest scraps of affection and, when they are finally tossed our way, convince ourselves these crumbs are a feast we can live off until the next time our beloved remembers we exist. But actually, we're starving.

Of course, in your case the boy finally did come around and ask you out, and you did get to experience that euphoric, miraculous time when you realize the person you love loves you back, that he's yours. But it sounds like even in the midst of this relationship, your depression never really went away. You wrote, "He never lost patience when I was up all night asking him why he was with me, because all I wanted to do was die. He slowly started to raise my self-confidence and I began to actually like the way I looked. I began to lose the suicidal thoughts, and he was with me through it all." And then when he wasn't around as much, "my depression hit hard and I felt suicidal again." That euphoria we feel when we're falling in love can temporarily override the blank numbness of depression, briefly waking us up and bringing us back to life, but it's not a real solution. You say this boy needed help as well, that he wouldn't let you "save him." What's more likely is that he knows, whether it's on a conscious or unconscious level, that you can't save him because it's impossible for anyone to save another person, no matter how much you love them. You can be supportive, you can be a source of strength, and you can comfort them when they are in pain. You can encourage them to seek help and listen as they process, but you can't save another person. Sometimes we want to believe that we can—that we're the only one who can—because it gives us a feeling of ownership, a special connection to the person we love. No one knows them like you do; no one loves them like you do, so no one can help them like you can. It's a heady feeling, but also a misguided one. You can't count on a boy to make you feel beautiful or make your suicidal thoughts go away. You need to learn how to cope, how to live with and love yourself during those times when you are not paired up with someone, either by being entangled in a messy friendship with fuzzy boundaries or in a proper "couple." The more you confront and deal with and treat your depression, the healthier and more successful your romantic relationships will be.

At the end of your letter you wrote, "And I don't know how to feel about it." Of course you do. You feel awful. You feel empty. You're grieving a loss. But you can't do nothing but feel your feelings all day long; that way madness lies. So, do other stuff, too. You may not want to get out of bed, much less leave the house; force yourself. Get your friends to come over, pull back the covers, and turn the light on. Or you can hole up in your bedroom writing maudlin poetry and listening to all the sad songs you know until you realize none of them accurately describe the way you feel and you're compelled to start writing your own songs. You can fill a sketchbook with a hundred drawings that all fail to authentically portray precisely how shitty you feel. Getting the shit kicked out of your heart once in a while is the price of admission for this whole human experience, and if you were to go through your whole life without ever feeling this kind of pain, you would be missing out on a huge piece of what makes you a person. The day will come when it is your turn to break somebody's heart, and having been on this end will remind you to do it compassionately and with empathy.

For a long time it will all be bad days—bad days and worse days, and it will feel like the world will be black and white forever. But one day that boy won't be the first thing you think about when you wake up. And eventually, you'll have a good day—you won't even notice at first, but you'll find yourself laughing with friends or absorbed in a great book, and you'll look up and realize you're thinking about him for the first time all day. The next day might be a bad one, but slowly the worse days will stop coming and you'll graduate from bad days and worse days to good days and bad days, and your world will gradually fill up with color again. When I was a freshman in college I was devastated by my first romantic disappointment. I had real hopes for this relationship, but he dropped out of school and moved back home, over a thousand miles away. Somehow it was worse that I couldn't even be angry; he'd done nothing I could fault him for, only what was right for him. I remember crying to a friend, "I can't do this," and her response has stuck with me for the twenty years since. "What do you mean, 'You can't do this'?" she said. "What is it you can't do? You're not going to stay in bed forever. You're not going to shrivel up and die. So you're already doing 'it,' the thing you say you can't do. You got up today. You went to class. All you have to do is keep doing it."

There's something singular about the way we love when we're young, before we start worrying about shit like how much money somebody makes or whether they want kids or if our parents get along with them. You say you were naive enough to believe you would marry this boy and you would be together forever. Maybe it was naive, but it was also brave and beautiful. It takes courage to love another person so fearlessly, especially after you've learned the hard way how much it fucking hurts to lose someone. It also takes guts to let somebody love you; it's hard enough to let yourself be seen and known, to own that kind of vulnerability, but to let somebody *love* you? To accept that love, to acknowledge you're deserving of it, is bold and radical and much easier said than done.

The next time you start to fall in love, will you stop yourself to avoid the possibility of getting hurt? Or will you let yourself surrender again, because this time love might last? Will your heart be ruled by hope or fear? I have a sneaking suspicion, dear Fireheart, that you're going to live up to your name.

Love,

Cristina Moracho

In my next life, I'm going to be an ass-kicking ninja warrior queen. And I will hunt shits like you down.

—*Bad Romance*, Heather Demetrios

Dear Heartbreak,

I fall in love with everyone, and it's a problem. It's like I see someone, anyone, and I can see their entire soul, you know? No matter how tired or sad or high they are, I can just kind of tell what kind of a person they are, what their heart looks like. Or part of it, I guess. This is a blessing and a curse because there's always another part to someone. There's always something they don't let seep through their skin. I didn't realize that not seeing all of someone could get me in trouble until it did.

There was this guy, and I thought I could see his soul, but it was wearing sunglasses. The kind of sunglasses that street racers wear. When he finally took them off, I could see his soul better, and his could see mine better, too. Everything looks better with a filter on it. He saw my soul and he saw that I was vulnerable and messed up and dependent and anxious all the time, and I didn't even realize I was being manipulated and taken advantage of until he literally punched me in the stomach

I'm better now, more or less. I'm more wary of people's souls. And I don't want that to be the case because I know that he's not all bad, either. Nobody is. So thanks, I guess.

—The Dragon Queen, 17

LOVE IS ALL, LOVE IS YOU

Dear Dragon Queen,

1. The ability to still love people after going through the mindfuckery of an abusive relationship is probably the most badass ninja-warrior shit a girl can do. I'd have you on my girl squad any day (who *doesn't* want a dragon queen on their squad?).
2. Falling in love with everyone isn't a problem. What *is* a problem is not falling in love with yourself. More on this later.
3. If I were to perform open-heart surgery on you (in this parallel universe, I'm a brilliant surgeon; don't worry), the first thing I would see in your heart is a hole. It might be no bigger than the size of a quarter. It might be the size of my fist. Since I'm not actually a surgeon, you're going to have to figure out how big that hole is on your own. And you're going to have to fill it. Also on your own. More on this later, too.

To answer your letter, I enlisted the help of my darling husband, Zach, who was there when I had to piece my heart back together after years of bad relationships, hurts at home, and other disasters. I've got lots to say to you, but I think it's really helpful to get a guy's perspective on matters of the heart, too. Especially a guy who filmed a documentary of my college production of *The Vagina Monologues* and thus has logged in countless hours hanging out with ladies who talk of nothing but heartbreak, vaginas, and how to take down the patriarchy. He's not one of those shitty guys whose eyes glaze over when you bare your soul, and he doesn't get all fidgety and try to change the subject. Also, I'm pretty sure that if he met your ex in a dark alley, he might be willing to set aside his general position of nonviolence. (I have no such position and so would happily kick your ex's ass, as long as he is a legal adult).

ON BEING A BADASS NINJA WARRIOR:

Heather:

The thing about loving people and seeing their souls and letting them see your soul is that sometimes you fall in love with a motherfucker. Life is unfair like that. I feel your letter so hard, Dragon Queen. I feel it because I was you when I was seventeen. My boyfriend didn't punch me in the stomach, but he was so manipulative, so verbally abusive, so jealous and controlling that one afternoon when I was home alone, I pulled a kitchen knife off the counter, sat on the floor across from the dishwasher, and had a long think about killing myself. It seemed easier than breaking up with him. Easier than facing the fact that I'd allowed my soul to be shredded to the point that I was willing to let it go. I felt just like you: vulnerable and messed up and dependent and anxious *all the time*. My boyfriend would spy on me at work, accusing me of flirting with customers, and once brought a baseball bat to one of my rehearsals for the school play, threatening to beat the shit out of a nice boy who had dared to be my friend. He made a point to say at least one scathing thing to me every day, mean little comments aimed at my self-esteem. I wasn't "deep" enough to understand his poetry, I was a wet blanket—a total drag to be around. I was selfish and slutty and didn't I know how much I was hurting him by talking to other guys? I was lucky to be with him—no one else, he said, would ever love me as much as he did. You see, I was so *hard* to love.

Lies. All of it. But it takes a while to see that.

Dragon Queen, we are not alone. Did you know that one out of every three teens is affected by teen dating violence? Did you know that there are girls all over the world *right now*, right this minute, whose boyfriends are beating them up physically, verbally, or emotionally? Some of these girls will go sit down on the floor with a kitchen knife. Some of them will use it. You, me, and every girl who doesn't use that knife—we're survivors. I tell you this so that you know that you are not weak. And it is not your fault that you were hurt like that. And also, I really wish I could punch him in the stomach for you. And knee him in the balls.

You talk about seeing other people's souls. Well, I see yours all over this letter. It is really goddamn beautiful. And brave. You've been through something crazy terrible and yet you're still open to the idea of love. Of connection. Of giving someone a chance. There are so many people who would close up shop after a relationship like yours. They'd hide behind walls, wearing armor all the time so that no one could see the real them. They'd wear blindfolds so they wouldn't be tempted into falling in love again. You don't want that. And *that's* why you wrote this letter. You want to keep yourself from building those walls and wearing that armor. That takes a big heart, guts, and a shit-ton of hope, all of which I think you have.

But you go one step further. Despite everything this boy did to hurt you, you're able to see that he's not all bad. I can't even begin to tell you how enlightened that is, that you can put aside your own pain and all the ugly in someone else and see a flicker of good. This gives me hope. Hope that you will be able to love again. Hope that you'll know when someone is worthy of the love you give, and that you'll know that you deserve all the love you receive—and then some.

But in the meantime, you have this heart that is broken. How do you fix it?

The answer is simple and so, so hard: Love yourself.

Zach:

Hey, Dragon Queen. Zach here. Thanks for writing your amazing letter. I agree with Heather about your badassitude, but I also want to recognize something else: Your radical heart-openness is not only badass, it's also *subversive*. There are Powers That Be who want you to shut down your heart, to squash your own sense of wonder at the possibilities of life. The system we live in wants good consumers, and a good consumer isn't a person who sees someone's entire soul and falls in love. Good consumers despair of ever finding love, or ever being worthy of it, and then go shopping and buy shit they don't need to fill the emptiness they are trying so hard not to feel (this is kind of like the "hole in your heart" that Heather mentions). I'm so glad you're not a good consumer.

More than that, it takes real *empathy* to see someone's soul and fall in love. What you're really saying is that you can see the beauty in people in spite of their insecurities, their fears, their self-destructiveness, or whatever other creeping things are hiding in the dark corners of themselves. You empathize with them because you can see some of those same things in yourself, too, and you choose to see their beauty in spite of all that. You choose to fall in love with them. What a magnificent choice. It isn't easy to make that choice. Don't ever stop falling in love with the world, Dragon Queen. Stay open and let yourself fall in love with everyone: the awkward clerk at the grocery store, the curiously well-dressed woman on the bus, the mail carrier rocking out with his headphones on. People are worth loving. They just are.

But . . . being empathetic—staying open to others—doesn't mean excusing their shitty behavior. I'm a husband now (Heather's, specifically—good choice on my part, right?), but before that I was just a regular old boyfriend. Heather and I started dating when we were eighteen years old, barely freshmen in college. By the time this book comes out, we'll have been married for fourteen years. That's a long time, and we are not the same people we were when we got together. We've gone through all kinds of changes and ups and downs, but one thing I'll say we have consistently done—even when we have disagreed—is treat each other with respect. Sometimes it seems like people talk about respect as though it's a lofty goal, like mutual respect is a state that only some select relationships eventually achieve while others are just "good enough." But that's not true. Respect is the bare minimum. Don't enter a relationship without it.

Respect means treating someone like they are valuable in and of themselves. It means *not* trying to get something out of them, or trying to change them, or being dismissive of them, or belittling their ideas. When you respect someone, you don't hurt them (I am *so sorry* this person hurt you, Dragon Queen), and you don't try to manipulate them—because you're not treating them as objects for your use. It sucks, but people, especially when they're young and still figuring themselves out, usually get into relationships for all the wrong reasons. You can fall in love with everyone and still be fiercely stingy about who you give your heart to. Don't give it to anyone who doesn't respect you—wait until they've removed those street racer sunglasses and you're sure they're worth it.

THE DEAL WITH SELF-LOVE:

Heather:

I don't remember when I started falling in love with practically every boy I encountered, but from the time my mind went all *THAT'S A BOY I WANTS IT* until I finally found the one I wanted to spend the rest of my life with, I lived in a state of pure, unadulterated anguish. Like you, I loved them all. Real boys. Fictional boys. Imaginary boys that hung out in my day-dreams. Boys in the supermarket. Boys sitting across a classroom, slouched in their chairs. Boys on roller coasters and surfboards and movie screens.

There were so many of these mysterious creatures; every time I encountered one, I would cut off a little sliver of my heart (and sometimes hack off a chunk) and proffer it on bended knee. *Do you want a piece of my heart? It's really good, I promise. Is best heart in all of America!*

See, as soon as I started noticing these boys, I started

seeing myself in relation to them. My identity became fractured and the value I placed on myself was all wrapped up in how these boys felt about me. Was I pretty enough? Smart enough? Cool enough? How could I get their attention and keep it? What did I need to do; who did I need to be so that they could *love, love, love* me?

I did this with girls, too. In fact, my friendships were the most intense romances of my life. Just like with the boys, I would fall head over heels in love with girls I had just met, girls who I wanted to be. They were my kindred spirits, sisters I became soul-bonded to over secrets and gossip and alliances. I lied for them, changed for them, fought for them. I betrayed myself, again and again, in order to stay in their good graces. *Please don't leave me alone with myself.*

I never had a moment when I thought: Why do I only have a good day if a boy laughs at my jokes and a girlfriend tells me I'm her *best* friend? Why do I only feel good about myself when other people feel good about me? Why am I giving these people the power to decide if I'm okay or not? It took me a really long time to start not giving a fuck. By which I mean, I began to see that it didn't matter whether I got others' approval or acceptance or love—I was never happy until I was happy with myself. (Full disclosure: still working on this—self-love is the deep end of figuring out how to human).

You said that you're "vulnerable and messed up and dependent and anxious all the time." I'm guessing that right now you might be having some difficulty seeing all the other parts of you.

I bet in addition to being vulnerable and messed up and dependent and anxious that you're openhearted and wonderfully complex and affectionate and thoughtful. I bet there are girls and boys that secretly watch you. How can they not, Dragon Queen? Someone that has a big enough heart to fall in love with everyone she meets *glows*.

Zach:

There's something that I hope you remember, Dragon Queen. The universe is 13.7 billion years old. And through the whole history of it—all the birthing and dying of stars, the formation of planets, the evolution of life from single cells to dizzyingly complex life, from the destruction of the dinosaurs to the rise (just *seconds ago* on a universal timeline) of the funny mammals we call humans—there has never been, and never will be, another *you*.

I know that sounds like a stupid cliché, and maybe it is, but most stupid clichés have at least a little bit of truth to them. Just think about that fact for a minute: No one has ever seen the universe through your eyes, and no one ever will. You're looking out at the world through the windows of your own secret, impenetrable tower. Every thought, perception, and experience you have is totally unique, because it's yours and no one else's. Because of your genes, the family you had or didn't have, the era and place you grew up in, the friends you had or didn't have, the people you've loved who may or may not have loved you back, your own successes and failures, joys and sorrows, and all the rest of the countless things that make up a person—*you* have a perspective on the universe that literally no one else does.

Wow! Does that fact feel frigging amazing to you? It should, because it's frigging amazing! So what does it mean? Well, think about this. The reason people pay so much for gold, or signed copies of a work of art, or limited-edition sneakers, is because those things are rare. Rare things are valuable. And if there's only one being in the entire history of infinity that sees the world through your eyes, then guess what? That makes you *infinitely* unique and valuable. Gold and sneakers got *nothing* on you.

But something tells me you already know this, Dragon Queen. If you're falling in love with everyone you meet, you already recognize how special they are. You say you're seeing their souls, but I think what you're really seeing is their infinite, shining uniqueness. For what it's worth, I'm going to make a new rule for you: You're not allowed to see that specialness in others unless you can see it in yourself. Sorry to get all authoritarian on you, but it's just not logical. How could *they* be beautiful and special and eternal if you're not? We're all on the same level with this whole being human thing we're involved in. No one is more valuable than you. That's deep, so I'll say it again: No one *on this entire planet* is more valuable than you. (Of course, you have to understand that this cuts both ways. No one is *less* valuable than you, either. It's a package deal, I'm afraid.)

Try this. Next time you look at yourself in the mirror, try not to see what you don't like. What's the point? You already know what you don't like about your appearance, anyway. Your teeth aren't straight enough, or you've got too many zits, or your bangs don't hang right, or one eye is just a little bit smaller than the other, or whatever. *Blah blah blabbity blah.* Forget all that shit that doesn't matter. Look at yourself the way you'd look at someone else when you fall in love with them. Instead of seeing someone else's soul, try to see your own for a change. Can you see it? Does it make you want to cry, to scream, to laugh? Does it make you fall in love with yourself? I hope it does, Dragon Queen.

I suppose it goes without saying that all of this is just my own unique perspective, right? Just the way I see it from my own impenetrable tower . . .

ABOUT THE HOLES IN YOUR HEART:

Heather:

Remember how I said that there's a hole in your heart? Well, there is. Don't worry; we all have them. The hole was in your heart before you fell for your boyfriend, and it will get smaller or bigger over the course of your life—its size, its whole *existence*, is up to you. If you work very hard on loving yourself, that hole may disappear entirely. The problem is, most people are pretty crap at loving themselves, and so they find other things they think will fill the hole: a boyfriend or dad, their job, school, trips to Target, awards, TV, whiskey. Spoiler alert: None of these things will do the trick.

These holes begin forming when we're really, really young. You didn't mention your home situation, Dragon Queen, but I'm guessing it might not be totally perfect. If it is, YAY! If not, then welcome to the club. Most of the human race are members.

My parents separated when I was three and divorced not too long after that. By the time I'd graduated from high school, I'd only seen my dad a handful of times in my life. The lack of a dad ripped a pretty big hole in my heart. It made me feel unloved. Like I wasn't worth sticking around for. My mom later marrying a dude my best friends and I took to calling Satan Incarnate made that hole bigger. By the time my abusive boyfriend came around, I was desperate for someone to come in and plug that shit up. And for a while, it seemed like he had. He was sweet and romantic—all the swoony things. And then he wasn't. The hole got bigger. Our parents, or the struggles we have feeling invisible out in the big wide world, or all the things society tells us we should be, but aren't: These are the things that dig holes in our heart.

Most people spend their whole lives trying to fill the empty places inside them. They think buying something or loving someone or going somewhere or doing some cool thing will fill those abysses. Sometimes it seems like they do, at least for a little while. And then, bit by bit, or sometimes in a whole flood, those spaces will open back up and it's like you have ten empty swimming pools in your chest and your gut. You'll know this is happening when you feel all the things you mentioned in your letter: messed up and dependent and anxious. You'll feel vulnerable, too, but vulnerable is good—it says you're still in the game, you've still got something to lose. When you're vulnerable, you become a truth teller, and that's as awesome as a badass ninja warrior.

We feel all those thorny things inside us when we're looking outside ourselves for confirmation of our worth. People loving us—or saying they love us—is usually how we determine if we're okay. We reason that if our boyfriends or parents or friends love us, then we are worthy of love, and thus we have value. But what if they stop loving us? Or they never loved us to begin with? Or they are so caught up in their own problems that they don't know *how* to love other people? And don't forget: The people you're hoping will fill you up have holes that need filling, too. And maybe they can help fill some of yours and you can help fill some of theirs, but that's not always the case, is it? My dad left—no love to fill that hole. Bad boyfriend? The hole gets bigger. Friends betray you? Goodbye, self-worth. You see where I'm going with this? The kind of unshakable love you need, the love that will be yours *no matter what*, can't come from other people. It starts with you. It ends with you. Anything in between— finding your true love, having a mom that rocks, knowing you have a girl squad you can depend on—this is all gravy.

I know, I'm sorry. But that's the shitty, grown-up truth. It might sound cynical, all lone-wolf I-don't-need-anybody, but that's not what I mean. Of *course* we want to love other people and love them well. We want strong relationships and we want to be loved—and we are *deserving* of love. Love from other people is good! Yay, love! But you won't even be able to enjoy or truly accept that love until you know you're worthy of it. And you won't know you're worthy unless you love yourself (remember how Zach said how freaking awesome you are because no one like you has ever existed in the entire cosmos?). Bonus: When you aren't expecting the people around you to carry shovels to fill the hole in your heart with their love and attention and praise, then you let the people you love off the hook. They don't have the enormous responsibility of holding your entire sense of worth in their hands. This is what we call a win-win situation.

Besides, Dragon Queen, you don't need anyone to tell you that you're kick-ass. You *are* kick-ass. You always have been. I want you to make a list of all the reasons you're awesome. Then read that list every morning. Add to it as your awesomeness increases. This knowledge that you are enough *just as you are* is what fills that hole. Our absent dads or dismissive mothers or traitorous best friends or boyfriends with clenched fists are the ones digging the holes. We're the ones that fill them back up. Here's some more homework: Listen to "Because" by the Beatles. This song came to mind while I've been sitting with your letter because it's a song with a heart as big as yours. *Love is all, love is you.* It's all you, Dragon Queen.

Zach:

Oh, the hole in the heart—how it aches in its emptiness! How the wind whistles through it like a lonely desert canyon!

How it palpitates like an exposed nerve, pulpy and quivering and raw! Yes, Heather is right (she's pretty much right about everything—don't tell her I said that or she'll get a big head and my life will be *unbearable*): The hole most definitely exists. It's part of being a person. It comes with the territory. You might even say it's our defining characteristic. We are the-creatures-with-holes-in-their-hearts. Buddha, in his no-bullshit-allowed way, just cut to the chase and made it the first of his Four Noble Truths: Life is suffering. (If that sounds way harsh, it's worth knowing that other English interpretations soften the blow a bit. "There is suffering in life," and "Life is unsatisfactory," are possible alternative readings.) No matter how you phrase it, though, it's still important enough that Buddha made it the starting point for everything else he wanted to teach. It's like he said, "Okay, life hurts. Something is always not quite right about it, nagging at you like a pebble in your shoe. There's no way around that. Can we just agree this is true and move forward? Great. So then . . ."

What to do about it—ah, that's the question. We can start by recognizing that the hole is there. That's a big first step. Tons of people just pretend that they don't notice its nagging, gnawing pulse. They push it away in all the ways Heather mentioned—and by quite a few other creative methods, as well. The most common is probably by throwing themselves at another person, hoping someone else has the missing piece that fits *just right*. They don't. Nobody has that for anyone else.

There's a movie from the '90s called *Jerry McGuire*. It has

Tom Cruise in it (don't get Heather started on Tom if you know what's good for you—her obsession with the guy is frankly a little spooky). Anyway, Tom's character is making a classic Big Romantic Speech to his love interest near the end of the film— the kind where our lovelorn hero confesses his true feelings, his pleading eyes glistening with trademark Cruiseian sincerity— and he tells the woman, "You *complete* me." Cue the tears and the pounding of hearts from coast to coast. The scene is undeniably romantic. It's also, not to put too fine a point on it, complete and utter horseshit.

Listen, Dragon Queen, I love my wife with everything I've got, and I know she loves me the same way. We're a damn fine team—we work and play and travel and scheme and laugh and couch-potato-out together like nobody's business. We inspire and challenge each other to be the best versions of ourselves. We're as compatible and complementary as it's possible for two people to be. But do we *complete* each other? Not a chance. And that's okay. Life is too untidy for that. Remember the first Noble Truth?

The hole in the heart doesn't disappear just because you've met the right person. Once you can honestly admit you've got it, though, you're ready to begin the important work of figuring out what the dang hole is *for*. It's not there for nothing. If you look closely enough, in fact, you'll see it's not really a hole at all. If you can step back from trying to fill it every second of your life (maybe by being a good consumer, maybe by settling for partners who don't respect you ...) it reveals itself to be a *tunnel*—a secret passageway to the heart of your heart. It's how you let people in, how you can empathize with them. Heather already talked about how important it is to stay vulnerable, and she's right again (as usual! How annoying!). The hole in your heart can end up being the same opening through which you fall in love with the world.

There's a saying Heather and I both love, from one of our favorite TV shows, *Friday Night Lights*. The characters would say this before they went out to play football, a kind of mantra that got them in the zone. Neither of us are sports people, but this has become a phrase that fires us up. We hope, Dragon Queen, that it will fire you up, too.

Clear eyes. Full hearts. Can't lose.

Love,

Only skin, muscle, and bone separate my heart from [his] heart. I am so close to him that I can feel it beating against my own chest.

—*American Street*, Ibi Zoboi

Dear Heartbreak,

I don't believe we've met before. I'm—well, if I tell you who I am you might be able to find me, which I'd like to avoid for now. I'm writing to you because, while I'd like to put off our inevitable meeting for as long as possible, I'm a little upset that we haven't even had the chance to become acquainted. I'm the type of person who craves love in all its forms—I want to have someone in my life that I can be my authentic self around. I want to find someone who I can sit in silence with, listening to the rain and the sound of our heartbeats. The problem is, that seems like an impossible task.

Every time I see someone that I want to meet, or want to get to know, my mind puts up a wall. "Why would they want to talk to *you*?" My brain and heart want love, but my mind puts its overanxious foot down. Someone reaching out to me is a welcome thought that I pray for every time I walk down the street with my earbuds in, but no one ever does. I feel pain, an ache deep down in my heart every time I let someone walk away with nothing but a hopeful smile, or force myself into not sending a text or email to a friend I desperately want more with, because I tell myself I would just be a burden to them.

Heartbreak, maybe I have met you after all.

Thanks for listening.

—Anonymous

KNOCK DOWN THOSE WALLS

Dear Anonymous,

Who placed those bricks around your heart? Did you ask for those walls to be there between that thing beating in your chest and whatever is on the other side of happy? The thing about walls is that you can knock them down. You can punch through them if you're angry. And if you still want them there, around your heart, you can paint them if you need a change of scenery, or you can hang a painting. You can stare at them all day, but the problem with that is they'll start to slowly close in on you. Walls can break you, too. They can knock you down. So can love.

But love is not like a brick wall. It's more like an ocean wave. Yes, it can knock you down; you can be swept off your feet. But unlike walls, it ebbs and flows. You can swim in it. It can carry you to new heights. But if you have a wall around your heart, the waves of love will only crash along its surface, never reaching the shores of your most beautiful, brilliant self.

So here is how to knock down the walls around your heart, of which there are plenty.

Things you will need:

A heart.

Warm, gooey feelings.

Words. Soft words. Sweet words. Gentle words.

Eyes. Warm eyes. Kind eyes. Deep, all-knowing eyes.

And hands. Preferably warm, too. And dry.

Imagine your heart beating behind a series of walls. No one can hear or feel its rhythm. It can't go out, as they say, to anyone. There's no heart-to-heart. It can't even break or ache because of all those walls.

Now, when you knock down that first wall, the whole universe will open up to you: outer space, the alignment of the planets, the waning and waxing moon, the stars at night, the clouds and sun in the day, and even the thunderstorms. Step outside and pay attention to how all these things move around you, whispering sweet everythings into your ear. The soft summer breeze is a poem. The raindrops are melodies to a love song. Even the harsh winter winds are a shout from the universe telling you that the Love of Your Life is standing at a bus stop shivering, with hands shoved into coat pockets, lips chapped, cheeks red, toes frozen, waiting for you to come and say something, anything.

So by taking a step toward this cold someone with questioning eyes, you remove another wall. Take a step toward them. Just one is fine.

It's okay if you only make eye contact and the words don't slip from your mouth as easily as you would've liked. So you

228

stand there with your own hands in your coat pockets, shivering, lips chapped, cheeks red, and the first snowflake lands on the tip of your nose and you brush it away. So Love of Your Life turns to you with those same questioning eyes, and that half-smile is another nudge from the universe. Smiles belong to the world beyond the clouds, too.

You look away because those stupid walls keep you from reaching out and touching back with your own smile. But the universe is still a wide, all-knowing place and it sends you another sign. Love of Your Life is not getting on the same bus, after all. These walls that stand between your heart and other people are well-placed and stubborn—you have to make a quick decision: You can either be late for school, or be on time for your fast-beating heart that feels as if it's about to leap out of your chest. Your heart is beating so fast that your legs don't move. You're frozen there, not from the cold, but from those stupid walls. They force you to stay behind as the bus leaves and it's just you and Love of Your Life on that cold Tuesday morning.

The most important things needed in knocking down walls around hearts are eyes. You need two sets. One for seeing and one for being seen.

Do Love of Your Life's eyes look away? Do they stare back? Are they cast down? Do they smile?

Does it matter? Because your own eyes glance, then cast down, then look about. Uncertain.

This is when most people choose to step away from the

wall. They let it sit there only seeing the glimmer of sunshine above the top and never moving close enough to feel its warmth.

The distance, the cold air, the moving cars, the naked trees don't stare back at you. They laugh at you because everything in that moment is telling you to knock down that wall, and you don't.

Out of the corner of your eye, you see that Love of Your Life has moved on to something else: a phone and the world that lives within it. You can look freely now. Boots, pants, coat, hair. But neither of those things makes you want to knock down those walls. It's the eyes. You need to see the eyes again. And the face that belongs to them. Most importantly, it's the smile that will send you over the moon and you'll come crashing down in seconds, hopefully landing on a stupid wall.

Walls are held up by the unrelenting ground like a forced group project. So you'll need more than just eyes to pry some of them apart. Words will do the trick. Start with hello. No. Too easy. Too revealing.

Time is always on your side. So ask Love of Your Life what time it is.

You already knew the time. And something about your eyes tells this truth about you. And Love of Your Life picks up on it, so the time doesn't end there. A brick has been pushed out of its place. There is indeed a hole now, so you peek.

Love of Your Life's eyes glance again, taking a quick note of your boots, pants, coat, hair. You hope that everything is in place, as it should be—glowing, shiny, and perfect. You scan your memory for words that aren't about the time. Place is a good start.

The town, block, school, grade. You want to know exactly where your heart will roam once that last wall comes tumbling down. You want to know what two points on the infinite map of fate have brought you both here.

The town is not so far. The block is even closer. The school is yours. The grade is the one above yours. There are many points of entry here. So the walls fall one by one to reveal the eyes again, and that precious beloved smile.

But this is all too much. Your heart races because it feels naked, exposed. Anything can happen at this point. Eyes can look away. Words can become rushed, then hushed. You take too long with your own words. Your eyes are the first to look away. You search the snowy ground for broken pieces of concrete from fallen walls. You need to stack them back up.

I have been here before, many times. I know what this feels like. And it wasn't always about someone I thought could be the love of my life. This wall is like the first day of school, the big test that I need to take to get into a good high school, or the move into my dorm room for college. It is basically fear. For whatever reason, I've always imagined the scary thing behind a wall was a steep cliff, and if I knocked down that wall, I'd fall to my death. Starting over in a new grade is scary, so I think, *I will die.* That test is hard. *I will die.* I'm moving out on my own. *I will die.*

If I like that person, and they don't like me back, and they're not the love of my life after all, *I will die.*

I did not die in any of these cases, and you won't, either. But you already know that. And besides, even if there is a steep cliff on the other side of that wall, it doesn't mean that you have to jump. Step back. Breathe. That wall is gone, so enjoy the scenery.

Love of Your Life is staring at the back of your head, enjoying the scenery. You can feel it, and in that moment, you feel even more exposed, naked.

Words are the first thing to knock those last few remaining walls. They're not your words, thank goodness. Love of Your Life shares words with you. They're about school. This is a great entry point. The words are questioning, so you answer each one with confidence. Biology. Mr. Turner. Third floor. AP English. Swim team.

This doesn't hurt. Not yet. You know heartbreak might be around the corner. You've been here before, that time when you knew nothing about walls around hearts. You were born bare, trusting and loving deeply. And with each small heartbreak—a checked-off "I don't like you," a casual "This isn't working out," or the harshest of them all, "No"—walls were put up.

Still, you make small talk and it all feels brand-new like September, or clothing tags, or laundry fresh from the dryer. All of these are fleeting.

But, again, the thing about walls is that they block your view. Your heart needs to see first in order to feel. Even if this moment passes, those eyes, that smile, the cold wind on your cheeks, the small talk will be stamped in your memory.

Good memories keep the heart from growing cold, keep walls from going up. Don't give too much power to bad memories—walls, falls, and breaks. They will cloud everything, even this moment when you are so free—naked, exposed—that your heart is like the beaming sun melting every cold, beautiful thing around the both of you.

The small talk turns into big talk with longer questions. These words make you think about yourself, the universe, and your place in it. These are things you've never talked about before.

This Love of Your Life has stepped into your side where these walls used to be, slowly taking space in your heart. And you have stepped into that heart, too. And it's okay. Stay there for a while. Sit back, chill, and enjoy the view.

Whenever you do step back into your own space, for whatever reason, you will not be the same person. You'll have grown an inch or two, not in size, but in love. Love expands you. Honest, fearless love stretches you to the limits you didn't even know were there. There won't be any walls. You can run freely and love freely. Your heart will not only beat, it will make music.

With love,

I want to know if we are the same, in the moments
when we're stripped bare.

—The Careful Undressing of Love,
Corey Ann Haydu

Dear Heartbreak,

People tell me that I'm too self-deprecating. They're right. The problem is that I just can't stop. No matter how hard I try, I can't seem to see any redeeming qualities that I may possess. Not when there are so many people who are so much smarter, prettier, more athletic, more social, and all-around better than me. I guess my lack of confidence is the reason why I've never been able to find a guy that pays me even the slightest bit of attention. It must be impossible for a guy to love a girl who can't even love herself. Honestly, though, I barely even notice or care about my lacking love life. There are simply too many other problems to worry about.

Maybe I chose the wrong friends. No, I'm not in with the drug dealers, or the social outcasts. My "friends" are the over-achievers. The ones who get straight A's, play two sports, and are active members of the stupid National Honor Society. Every day I sit at our lunch table and listen to talk about college, boy-friends, and fun weekend plans, which I am rarely invited to. Every day I sit there silently and absorb the happy chatter with disdain. The people who are supposed to be my biggest support-ers make me feel like a complete failure. They don't do it on pur-pose. To an outsider, I probably look like I belong. I probably look happy, but the truth is, I've never really fit in. Probably because I've never really been able to like myself.

When I was a little kid, only two or three years old, I started literally pulling my hair out. My worried parents ordered me to stop with constant reminders, so I did. For a while. When the stress of middle school hit me, I started pulling again, and I couldn't stop. I hid my shameful behavior from parents and friends, but was old enough to understand that what I was doing was abnormal. I did some research. Turns out that hair-pulling is actually a fairly common impulse-control disorder called trichotillomania. It may affect up to four percent of the population, but people don't talk about it. It holds the same stigma as mental illness and is closely linked to anxiety. For me, it certainly is a coping mechanism for stressful situations. Still, it feels shameful, so I do my best to hide it from everybody. I spend every day trying to blend into the crowd. The last thing I need is one more thing to identify me as weird, and possibly slightly crazy. Everything's connected—my concealed secrets, painful shyness, and intense self-deprecation. No wonder I can't seem to find romance.

Sorry, Heartbreak. That was a bit of a rant.

—A Secretly Unhappy Teenager

OPEN THE DOOR AND WALK THROUGH IT

Dear Secretly Unhappy Teenager,

Sometime around the beginning of high school, I developed a strange habit. When I was upset I would dig my fingernails into the skin at the base of the palm of my hand. If I was extremely upset, I would bite that same patch of skin. There wasn't a *why* for the behavior, just an instinct that the feelings of depression and anxiety and fear and loneliness were too much for the insides of my heart and had to travel to other expanses of my body. The habit never turned into something more serious. I didn't go toward razors or matches or anything else to hurt myself. Only once did I manage to draw blood. But it was a secret.

There were other secrets, too. An ongoing experiment to see how long I could go without eating before someone noticed. When I realized the answer was, more or less, forever, I wasn't really sure what to do, so I coaxed out a lackluster relationship with cheese sandwiches and called it a day. There was a sick parent on the sofa. There was a nightly cry in my bed, where I wondered at the depth of loneliness, how vast and strange it was, how relentless. *I'm the only person I can trust*, I would whisper to myself, and it felt more than true. It felt real.

There was the group of girls who turned from best friends to enemies seemingly overnight. They were the overachievers, too. They were the smart ones, with good grades and big collections of books in their bedrooms and sharp wits and photographs of their parents at fancy colleges hanging in their living rooms. With them, I felt I belonged. I wasn't quite an overachiever—I never mastered the art of getting A's—but I loved books and I didn't think I'd be able to pull off partying and I loved our weekly Friday-night sleepover where we watched movies and talked about everything we hated and loved about being twelve and thirteen and fourteen. They were a safe space, away from the sometimes confusing dynamics of my family life and the strange weight of depression hanging in my home.

One night, at a ninth-grade dance at a nearby school for boys, I met a cute boy. He was a hockey player, short and stocky. He smelled like he'd chewed about forty sticks of gum before grinding with me on the dance floor. He grabbed my butt. No one had grabbed my butt before, and I didn't hate it. Other guys had tried before, but it was the sort of thing I didn't want to have just anyone do. I'd always told them no before. This time I pulled closer to him to let him know it was okay. I was excited to tell my friends. None of them were really dancing with anyone, but I was sure they would, soon. And when the time came, I would pick out cute guys or girls for each of them. I would happily giggle over their butts getting grabbed.

After a few dances, Jane, my red-haired best friend, tapped me on the shoulder. "Let's step outside for a minute," she said. Russ, the cute hockey player/butt-grabber, teased me about not wanting me to go anywhere, about wanting another dance, and I was flushed with excitement and nerves and Best Night of My Life-ness. I told Russ I'd be right back, and I followed Jane to the hallway outside the cafeteria where the dance was going on. All my best friends were already sitting on the floor in that hallway, waiting for me. They'd saved me a space in the circle. As soon as I sat down they started a conversation that had clearly been planned for weeks without my knowing it. They told me they were disappointed in me. That I wasn't the person they used to know. That I was superficial and boy-crazy and changing too much, too fast. They told me I wasn't really their friend anymore; I wasn't the kind of person they wanted to be friends with. I wasn't the kind of person they thought I was.

The night moved so quickly from wonderful to terrible, I could barely process what they were saying. There was a sleepover scheduled at my home for after the dance, and I still wanted to spend more time with Russ and I didn't understand what I was doing in that hallway of that school, listening to the last few songs drifting out from the cafeteria. I cried my eyeshadow off. It was fine—I didn't really know what I was doing with eyeshadow anyway.

The girls stayed over at my house that night. We pretended everything hadn't shifted. We took pictures that I still have in an album somewhere. All of us being silly, lighthearted, together, best friends. I was a little broken and a little relieved. Maybe this happened in friendships. Maybe I had imagined how bad it was. Maybe, just maybe, nothing really had to change.

Come Monday, it was over. I was frozen out. I was done.

No apologies came. No further conversations occurred. I went from being a girl with friends to a girl without.

Is this when the nail digging began? Is this when I lost my appetite, when I started wondering if anyone cared? Maybe.

Did anyone notice? No.

When I spoke to adults about it—parents, guidance counselors, anyone who I thought might tell me how I was going to survive the next week, month, year without friends—they sided with the other girls. The smart, accomplished ones who didn't wear much makeup and weren't hooking up with any boys. They asked me to think about my actions, about what I might have done to deserve their treatment of me. This was before the days of slut-shaming, before that term meant something that made people's heads nod with understanding. But that's what it was.

They dismissed the girls' cruelty and expected me to apologize.

Later, there would be other adults. I would tell them the story and they would get it. They would see the way the words had shaken me, had even maybe destroyed some essential part of me. Those adults knew I wasn't just a blond girl with big boobs and short skirts. Those adults saw the Something Else that all of us have beneath the way we wear our hair and the shade of lipstick we choose and the exact size and shape of our bodies.

I wish I had known to go to those adults.

I wish I had learned more quickly how to tell the difference between people who saw my outside and people who saw something further in. Something Else.

I wasn't sure what I would apologize for. I didn't know quite what I'd done wrong. Or, rather, I'd decided that what was wrong was simply me. *I* was wrong. They didn't approve of me. Because the things I'd done—worn makeup, flirted with a hockey player, blabbered on a little too much about boys, cared a little too much about what those boys thought of me—seemed so normal, the only thing that made sense was that it wasn't my *actions* that these girls hated so much as some intangible but vital part of my being. I was pretty sure lots of girls all over the world liked boys and experimented with blush and showed skin. So the thing that was awful and insurmountable and unworthy about me must be . . . just me.

How could I apologize for being myself?

I never got those friends back. I never made many friends at all for the rest of high school. I dated boys. Serious, long-term relationships that practically drowned me.

One of them shook me, sometimes, when I was especially annoying. He called me slutty when he didn't like what I was wearing. He made sure I knew the sacrifice he was making being with someone as damaged and bad as me.

He sounded a lot like those long-ago friends.

At the time, I thought that if more than one person thinks something about you, maybe it's true. That's what it's easy to tell yourself, late at night, in a twin bed in Massachusetts, in a nice house on a nice block that is so quiet all you could ever hear are crickets. Because I knew for sure *I* wasn't a person who could be trusted, I wasn't worthy or good or special or smart. My opinion about who I was didn't matter. Because *I* didn't matter. And because of how little I felt like I mattered, whoever entered the room, whoever had an opinion on me—well, they must be right. They must know more than me.

I was still trying to untangle who I actually was. Was I the girl at that dance, disappointing her friends? Was I the girl before that, whose friends seemed to love her? Was I the girl with the nice boyfriend everyone knew, or the girl with the boyfriend who treated her like crap? Was I the girl who smiled when someone told me to smile, or was I the girl who dug her fingernails into her hands and wished those stupid crickets would just shut the hell up?

To this day, the sound of crickets makes me lonely.

Here's what it looked like on the outside:

I was pretty. Pretty in the easy way. Blond-haired and blue-eyed and petite with huge boobs and teeth made perfect by braces. I had a dimple. I liked short skirts and high heels. I got auditions for commercials outside of school. I was a textbook model, laughing at a math worksheet in a stock photo in your geometry textbook. I did a commercial for a local mattress store. Everyone thought I would make it, someday, as an actress. I was set. I lived in a big house in a nice town and had my own phone line in the days before cell phones. I learned how to do my hair (sort of) and I bought sweaters from the right stores.

I had a series of boyfriends starting right at the beginning of ninth grade. During the Valentine's Day rose drive, one of the more serious of my boyfriends got me a dozen red roses instead of just one. Even the senior girls were talking about how romantic it was.

And it was romantic. But so much of romance at fourteen is being able to tell your friends about it. And I had no friends to tell.

Boys talked about my boobs, my butt, sometimes maybe even my face. I was cast as the lead in the high school musical even though I was only a freshman.

I'm sure it looked easy. I made it look easy. Or at least I made it look fine. I made it look like a life I had chosen.

But that exterior life, the one everyone saw, meant nothing to me. It wasn't real. My real life, the one I was living and suffering through and trying to survive, was the only life I could feel. It was the only life I had an actual connection to. My life, my world, was the secret one, the one I was working hard to hide. The biggest thing I felt, the most impressive feeling, the one bowling me over every day, was shame.

Like your shame, it was a secret shame. Invisible to anyone

giving me a passing glance. I was hiding so much from so many people, it's hard to say how I ever managed to get through a single hour without passing out from the pressure of that shame and those secrets. Above all else, I hated myself. I hated what a bad job I was doing at being happy, I hated how impossible it was for me to feel anything remotely close to okay, and I hated how easy being alive looked for everyone else. I even hated the way those sweaters looked on me, and I was sure they looked better, more effortless, on the other girls wearing them.

Everything looked effortless on other people. I was jealous of them. And lonely. So, so lonely in how hard being normal was. In the effort it took to pull off Normal Teen Girl.

Years later—last year, in fact—I was listening to the radio. A classmate that I didn't know well had a show on a popular radio station. She was speaking about how high school was for her and her family. She described pain I knew well—mental health struggles within her family, shame, secrets, complicated things that no one could know about.

The now-woman used to be one of the girls I dreamed about being. She had long, straight hair and an easy way of wearing clothes that made her look chill and pretty and fun and at ease with herself and the world. I remember her laugh and how beloved she was. One of the popular girls that even the unpopular girls liked. One of those special, charismatic people who get everything handed to them so easily, who didn't struggle or falter or find themselves embarrassed or alone.

Except, of course, that wasn't the whole picture.

I imagined, listening to her story on the radio, an alternate timeline of high school, another version of events. In this alternate universe, she and I both got tired of secrets around mental health issues and complicated family lives, and spoke openly about what was going on behind the pretty surface of the lives we presented. In this alternate reality, we named the things going on inside us and inside our family members. We called anxiety *anxiety* and depression *depression*. We found comfort in the ways our lives had shared secrets and shared pains, and we found a way to talk about those things so much, so often, with so much clarity, that they stopped having power over us.

In this alternate reality, we are two teen girls having a really hard time, who have a space to talk about it with someone else who gets it. In this alternate reality, those things—those terrible, secret, shameful things—seem a lot less terrible, because someone who looks good in sweaters and has a great laugh and seems one hundred percent "normal" has the same problems.

In this alternate reality, things are just a little bit easier, and I am just a little less likely to dig my fingernails into the palm of my hand, a little less likely to skip dinner, a little less likely to cry myself to sleep at night.

There are some people for whom high school really is easy. I believe that to be true. (I also know, with the certainty that time provides, that other times will be less easy for them.) But there are so many people—even perfect-looking ones, even easygoing ones, even admired and envied ones—for whom high school is filled with secret shames and terrible truths. And the only way to find your way to those people is to start opening up about yourself.

I will never forget sitting in the car with my husband, listening to the radio and hearing the story of a girl who was at the same tiny school as me for an entire six years talk about a life so much like mine. I will never forget the feeling of loss I had, that I could have been less lonely, had one of us broken through the shame and owned our stories. If I could change anything about high school, it would not be grinding with Russ and enjoying him grabbing my butt. It wouldn't even be dating that terrible guy or biting the palm of my hand. If I could change anything, I would change that it was all a secret. I would have owned my story. I would have taken the things that scared me most, and found safe people to be honest with them about. I would have said, "I am struggling with anxiety. I am struggling with some self-harm. I have a boyfriend who isn't safe. I have a parent who isn't well." I would have tried harder to own those things, and to take comfort in the moments of connection that inevitably come from opening up and sharing the most vulnerable bits of yourself.

In my life now, I speak about my problems openly. It happened slowly. I wrote a book about OCD, and I got asked questions about my own mental health. It became easier to say "I struggle with anxiety" than to pretend it away. At some point, it simply gets easier to be honest.

And with that honesty comes power. When it's something you own instead of something you fear, it's less shameful. And

strangely, the more I talk about my own mental health struggles, or the struggles within my family, the more people come
forward with their own. Once that door opens, people walk
through it. Once that door opens, everyone can breathe a little
easier. Once that door opens, it's a little less lonely.

I urge you to walk through the door.

I urge you to walk through the door as soon as you can,
because as far as I know, it's the only way out.

Walking right there beside you,

Sometimes you make choices in life and sometimes choices make you.

—*If I Stay*, Gayle Forman

Dear Heartbreak,

I have never felt your abuse as others have. Given that I am seventeen years old and have not yet liked someone in a romantic way or even had a crush on anyone, I've never been tormented by you, nor felt your pain. I've never cried my eyes out or eaten my feelings away because someone I loved didn't love me back. I've never gone through weeks of depression to get over a breakup, and I've never felt that horrendous ache in my chest at knowing that my love had been wasted, used up on someone who couldn't even return the favor. In all my years, I've never felt your fiery hand upon my cheek, or collapsed beneath your harsh words. But I've also never gotten that fluttery feeling in my stomach that I've been told people get when they fall in love. I've never had any kind of romantic relationship with anyone, I've never heard the words "I love you" in a romantic way. I've never had one smell, one jacket, that I've loved more than all the rest, nor have I stayed up all night thinking about a special someone. I've never had a single person in my life that I could share a special, unique love with. I haven't even had my first kiss. This is all because you're like a clingy, abusive boyfriend who refuses to let me get close with anyone of the opposite gender, and you control me with threats of violence. It's what you do to everyone.

Our relationship, Heartbreak, is toxic. You threaten me with pain and depression, and I bow down to your wishes and allow you to retain your control over me. You raise your hand, and I cower—too scared to risk confronting you or your sick ways. I'm so afraid that something bad might happen that I give up experiencing the best feelings that this world has to offer. Even now, I walk down the hallways at my school with my nose stuck in a book because the realities in the pages are much better than the ones in real life. In these fictional stories, the characters, more often than not, have these perfect relationships based on love at first sight, then they spend the rest of their days living happily ever after together. These realities are the ones that I grew up learning about, the ones that I fell in love with. Everyone in these fictional worlds has perfect love lives, because you do not exist there. It's all love and almost no heartbreak, and even when you do rear your ugly head, love still prevails. The pair work out their problems and banish you from their world. It's the way it should be.

However, in the real world, you plague most people with insecurity, self-doubt, and fear. In the real world, you control the girl who rants about all the bad things her boyfriend does every day, the boy who takes his own life because his girlfriend broke up with him, and even the one who won't open up to anyone because she was violated. I see you in more places than I want to and I can see the knife that you have placed right above everyone's heart, threatening to plunge deep if they get too close to another. I know that you make love not nearly as pleasant as it seems to be. There are ups and downs, guys who use girls, and girls who tear out guys' hearts. I am terrified of being caught in the middle of that. I am terrified that, because of you, the first guy I fall in love with isn't going to love me back because I don't have a tiny waist, a flat stomach, or perfect hair like the media says girls need to have. I'm scared that I'm going to reach out, make myself vulnerable for the first time ever, and he'll just look at me like I'm crazy, like there's no way that he could ever like me. I am afraid that any guy I have a crush on is going to shove you in my face faster than anyone around me can warn me about the jerk I decided to love. I am scared of you because you exist, and so I want to protect myself and my fragile heart from the abuse that you threaten if I step out of line.

Yet at the same time, I want to fall in love, and I want to experience that fluttering feeling. I want to have someone special in my life, someone who's more than just a friend. Nevertheless, you're determined to keep me away from love. Your abusive ways continue to scare me, Heartbreak. I want to experience romance, but you hold me back. You have held onto me for my entire life, and I don't know when you're going to let me go. But no more, Heartbreak. Here I say, *No more.* I am done sacrificing one of the best things in the world to avoid your anger. Living in fear of you is not living. Life requires risk, and I am ready to risk my heart to be able to love. I will no longer allow myself to be scared of your threats, and the chance that I might feel your abuse. If you decide to lay it on me, then so be it. I can take it. I am tired of being afraid of you. I am tired of living in the prison that you have created for me. Therefore, I'm breaking up with you. No longer will you be my abusive, controlling boyfriend. No longer will you keep me from reaching out and taking a chance. I am not yours. You, Heartbreak, do not have any control over me anymore. I am breaking up with you. And there is nothing that you can do about it.

Love,

Confident, 17

THE TEACHER OF ALL THINGS

Dear Confident,

I must inform you that I think your letter got lost in the mail. The letter you have written is to Heartbreak, but really, the entity to which you are speaking is Experience.

Everything you write in your wrongly-addressed-to-heartbreak letter is really a beckoning call for experience. Even the fears before which you tremble—pain and rejection and heartbreak—are actually further proof of your deep desire for experience. Confusing, I know. Who wants pain and rejection and heartbreak? But I suspect you already know, Confident, that the good and the bad, the joy and the pain, are buy-one-get-one-free, like it or not. So the thing you crave and the thing you fear are one and the same. You want experience. You want life. You want more.

You are seventeen years old. I don't say this to you to minimize your wisdom. There's an adage that as babies, we are born knowing everything, and then we spend our lives forgetting. So at seventeen, you are so much closer to knowing everything than I am, so much more in touch with wisdom.

What I mean by you being seventeen is that your days in this world are relatively brief. You are a puppy. A spring pea. A cherry blossom. Your time on this planet is still so fresh. I know it might not seem like that, particularly on those lonely weekend nights when you feel the whole world is doing something amazing while you binge episodes of *Dance Moms*, or those dreary afternoons when you're dying for the final bell to ring. But trust me as someone who has been seventeen and is now no longer seventeen, you're still a relative newbie.

And you crave experience. You ache for it. You are practically turning yourself inside out with hunger for it. This fluttering you talk about, that's your inchoate desire for experience, beating its wings to get out of the cocoon. Right on time, I might add. Some of the milestones we impose on life are pretty arbitrary (Twenty-one to drink? Twenty-five to rent a car? Why, exactly?). But there is a reason that, at eighteen, you legally become an adult. It's because in body, mind, and spirit, you are evolving and changing. You are preparing to leave childhood behind.

Forgive me if the word *childhood* chafes or feels condescending. I don't mean it as such. I know at seventeen you've long since stopped feeling like some little kid. But those butterfly wings beating inside you, they prove my point. That's the adult in you, raring to go, right at the time the world is ready to open up to you in ways you maybe can't even imagine.

You are preparing yourself, not for what you don't want, but for what you do.

How am I so confident that you really meant to send your letter to Experience? Because you told me so. You told me by recounting the experiences you have not yet had—first kiss—and the experiences you are terrified of—broken heart. And the experiences you have enjoyed, sometimes frustratingly second-hand, through books. (Though I would beg to differ with your assertion that "everyone in these fictional worlds has perfect love lives, because you [heartbreak] do not exist there." As a creator of many of these fictional worlds, let me point out that heartbreak is always there, lying in wait, stalking like a deadly leopard. As authors, our job is to beat our characters with a misery stick until they bleed and our readers bleed for them.)

But I think what you're seeing in these fictional worlds, what you're perhaps envious of, is not the perfect love lives or absence of heartbreak, but the presence of such profound and intense experience.

And here I'm going to let you in on a little secret. Some of the books you read, some of the books I write, are kind of full of shit. Not that the emotions or characters or circumstances are untrue but that the likelihood of such intense and pure experience happening at the age of sixteen, seventeen, eighteen is small. And thank God for that. Great fiction seldom makes happy living. You have your whole life to experience immense joy and immense pain, the highs of love, the lows of heartbreak. It will happen. Take that as a promise or a threat.

Outside of books, there is little romance to having your initiation to loss and grief and tragedy come early. That you have not experienced tragedy yet—and perhaps you have, but since you didn't mention it, I'm going to assume you haven't—might make you feel dull or normal or unexceptional, but I'm grateful on your behalf. Maybe one day, you'll be grateful on your behalf, too.

I am not so old and unwise that I can't remember how it felt to be thirteen, walking around the mall, because, in suburbia, this is what we did, and I'd look around at the shops and the Valley Girls (I grew up in *that* valley) and the houses and feel a tug. The tug whispered: *There has to be more than this.* More than tract houses and swimming pools and Contempo Casuals and football games. My world felt small then and I was already beginning to outgrow it.

I started taking tiny explorations, spending hours each weekend at the local record store, where the music geeks took me in as some sort of mascot (a lucrative one; I spent all my money on rare vinyl Eyeless in Gaza imports no one else cared to buy). The record store was across the street from the mall, not two miles from my house, but it was a portal of sorts. I went through that portal and on to the next one, taking two-hour bus trips to Melrose Avenue, which back then was a haven of punk subculture, and from there to dark, smoky clubs, where I found further escape, more *more*, in music. I'd watch bands and come away ears ringing, heart bursting, desire about to breach its dam. Once after a Waterboys show, I took my mom's sewing shears and chopped off my hair because that desire for experience and truth and things I could not name was thrumming so powerfully inside of me, I needed some way to let it out.

I am not so old and unwise that I can't remember how it felt to be fifteen and desperate to fall in love. My friends had been doing this for years now, it seemed. I'd watched them fall into what we all decided were Forever Loves only to see those Forever Loves implode so dramatically and, my God, I coveted it all. I wanted all that emotion, all that devotion, all that feeling, even if it came with the shit. Or especially if it came with the shit. Pain was romantic, too. People wrote songs about pain.

I wanted love and, later, sex and the melding of the human heart, and in pursuit of that I fell in love, hopelessly, endlessly, dramatically, with a series of boys who did not know I existed. They did not know I existed because they were either rock stars (oh, that Bono was already married, such heartbreak) or fictional (Rochester was my first bad boyfriend) or friends of my older sister, guys who treated me like the kid that I was, and guys who likely had no idea that I was the one mailing them song lyrics. (*I may be young but I'm a whole lotta fun. Seriously.* I did that. You are the first person I have ever admitted that to.) Now that I cop to this publicly, it looks a bit like stalker behavior and in retrospect I don't know what I would've done had they responded—I was like a dog that chases cars; I had no clue what to do if I caught one, and luckily I didn't. But I wrote these letters and did these silly-in-retrospect things because my feelings were so big, so intense, I needed to pin them somewhere. I needed to imagine what it would feel like to catch a car so that when I did one day, I'd be ready to do whatever it is dogs do when they catch cars.

I am not so old and unwise that I can't remember how it felt to be nineteen, getting my first tattoo inked onto me by a beautiful Dutch man with perfect bone structure (maybe that's redundant; all Dutch men have good bone structure) who went by the name of Igor Mortis. I remember relishing the pain and being giddy afterward because that tiny tragedy-comedy mask on the outside of my right ankle felt like an insurance policy. At that age, I had begun to glimpse, even to touch and taste, the *more* I so desired, and I knew I never wanted to go back. The tattoo was tiny, big enough to horrify my parents but too small for anyone else to notice. But in 1988, when tattoos were still mostly the domain of bikers and rockers, it felt like a radical demarcation on my skin, a no-backsies before/after, a contract with myself that I would always pursue experience.

All of which is to say I fully understand your longing for more. It is an elusive thing to catch, particularly at seventeen when annoying adults are telling you to just slow down and enjoy your youth and be patient, but that's easy for them to say because they are not bursting out of their very skin, quivering like a racehorse at the gate, needing to break out of the safety of childhood and into the more perilous waters of adult life.

It's coming, Confident. It's coming. I promise you. Take that as a threat or a promise.

It's both, actually. Which is why it makes sense that you're scared. Of falling for the wrong person who will dump you. Of having your ego wounded because someone doesn't find you desirable. Of having your heart broken. And more scared of not having any of these experiences. I totally understand all those fears. Let me try to assuage some of them.

You will get your heart broken. You will be rejected. You will feel lonely and alone. You will experience pain.

Now, if this letter were really meant for Heartbreak, telling you that would be cruel and sadistic. But because I am fairly sure you're actually writing to Experience, I'm hoping it won't.

If you never felt hunger, Confident, you would never know the precise pleasure of satisfying your appetite with delicious food. If you never experienced rainy days, you would not relish the feel of the spring sun on your face.

Joy and pain are not unrelated. They are not opposites or mortal enemies. They are conjoined twins. If you know joy, you will invariably know pain. You will break up with someone you loved. You will be dumped by a dear friend. You will sit at the bedside of sick loved ones. You will attend funerals, some of them for people who died before their time.

This is the price of admission, my friend. If you want experience, you must accept it. And I know that's scary. Nobody wants to feel loss and hurt, and I'm not ever going to tell you that hurt is noble. Hurt is hurt. And it can hurt like a motherfucker.

But there's a mitigation to the pain. Once again, it comes in the thing you want: experience.

Experience will teach you that life is a wheel: Sometimes you're up, sometimes you're down. And wherever you are, it won't last.

Experience will prove to you that you are resilient. You can survive what might seem unimaginable. Experience will teach you that sometimes the worst things have unexpected grace.

Experience will show you that often we are strongest in our broken places.

It can also teach you about the person you want to be, the life you want to lead. How many times do you touch a hot stove before you realize it's not a good idea? How many times will you date a jerk before you decide you deserve better? How many times will you be dumped by a friend before you decide to find a different kind of friend? How many times will you second-guess your instincts before you learn to trust yourself?

These are questions I'm asking of you, and they are questions I continue to ask myself. The asking, and answering, helps me to grow and learn things about myself, to surround myself with the kind of people who will help me enjoy the sunshine and weather the storms.

Part of me wants to do that old-person annoying thing and advise you not to rush it, Confident. Not to be in such a hurry to escape the safe cocoon of childhood and burst in the more turbulent waters of adulthood. But I know this too is bullshit. Partly because I bet you're already in rough waters. Even if you have a seemingly good life—no illness, no abuse, no neglect, little discrimination, the usual amount of family dysfunction—I know how hard it can be at your age: pressures from school and parents, boredom, not to mention complex friendship dynamics (and sometimes, I wonder if all the angsty, mean drama of middle school and high school is a misguided desire for experience; drama is not actually the same thing as experience, but it can feel that way).

But as someone who was herself in a hurry, telling you to be patient would be hypocritical. My thirst was so immense that when I was sixteen, I went abroad to England for a year as an exchange student. That year was in many ways hard. I lived with a family I never felt entirely comfortable with. I was homesick. I had my heart broken. But it was a year of experience and I soaked it up like the dry Valley Girl sponge I was. It was the year that started me traveling. I've never quite stopped. (Side note: Travel is an excellent way to experience lots of, well, experiences.)

I was also in a rush to find a great love. I went through a lot of guys, or maybe they went through me, trying to find someone I could deeply love, who would love me in kind, who'd write me the kind of songs that made my heart burst. It just never seemed to work out. The guys I loved, the ones I threw my heart at, treated it cavalierly. The guys who liked me, the ones who on paper seemed so great—they'd write me poems or cook me dinner or decorate my car in flowers—made my skin crawl. I feared there was something wrong with me. That I would be forever out of sync, loving the wrong people, rejecting the right ones. I was scared I'd never find someone I loved who'd love me back. I'd never have a proper boyfriend. Spoiler: I did, three months shy of my twenty-third birthday. Which at the time felt geriatrically old to experience all those goofy milestones (one-month anniversary! exchange of house keys! moving in together!) but in retrospect seems so incredibly young to find the person you might maybe spend your life with.

So go ahead and be impatient. Go ahead and desire experience. In this way, you are making yourself ready for it. You are braving up for it. You are opening yourself up to it.

But you know this all already, don't you, Confident? Because by the end of your letter, you seem to understand that you've never been talking to Heartbreak. You acknowledge that to live life fully, to open yourself up to experience, is an inherently risky act because you are inviting joy and pain. They both show up at the table, hungry. You will wind up feeding them both.

At the end of your letter, you say you're breaking up with heartbreak. But this letter was never to heartbreak. So you're not actually breaking up with anyone. What you're doing is getting together. With experience.

May it be a lifelong relationship.

Yours,

Gayle Forman

xx

If you put each title of our letters together,
you get a poem. We wrote this just for you, to stick
in your back pocket and look at whenever
Heartbreak comes to visit.

BIGGER THAN HEARTBREAK

Who said I have to give my heart up for breaking?
I am tired of trying to prove my worth
We have to be who we are

We're not alone
If you call, I will answer
You are so far from broken
Bigger than heartbreak

Life in the friend zone?
Knock down those walls
How to find a boyfriend in your heart:
Down the rabbit hole and out the other side
Do you care to reside within?
Open the door and walk through it

Own your heart
Stay you
Grow wildly

Love is all, love is you
The teacher of all things

RESOURCES

Below are resources for those of you who find yourself in an abusive relationship—physical or otherwise. And for those of you who feel like complete and utter shit and could really use someone to talk to. And for those of you who feel lonely, invisible, unsafe, traumatized, or in any way scared. Know that there are so many people out there who want to help you, who understand what it's like to deal with the pain you have. Know that you matter. You're not alone. I hope our letters show you that.

**These hotlines are free, private,
and open 24 hours a day:**

National Suicide Prevention Lifeline: 1-800-273-8255

National Sexual Assault Hotline: 1-800-656-HOPE (4673)

National Domestic Violence Hotline: 1-800-799-SAFE (7233)

National Child Abuse Hotline: 1-800-4-A-CHILD (422-4453)

The Trevor Project Hotline for LGBTQ+young adults:
1-866-4-U-TREVOR (488-7386)

Love Is Respect Abusive Relationship Hotline:
1-866-331-9474

These are great organizations with super-helpful websites and tons of resources:

Love Is Respect (loveisrespect.org): If you're in an abusive relationship, this organization has your back. There are loads of resources on their site, including a quiz to see if your relationship is healthy. Peer advocates are available 24/7 if you need someone to talk to. Text "love is" to 22522 or call 1-866-331-9474.

Born This Way Foundation (bornthisway.foundation/get-help-now): Here you'll find help with PTSD, body issues, LGBTQ+situations, and more.

The Trevor Project (thetrevorproject.org): Crisis intervention, suicide prevention, and other help for LGBTQ+teens. Call the hotline (1-866-488-7386) or visit their website. They love you and want to help.

Girls Health (girlshealth.gov): This website covers it all. It's a really good place to visit if you have body issues, are struggling with drug and alcohol abuse, are dealing with bullying, or are concerned about your safety.

ACKNOWLEDGMENTS

Thank you to everyone who submitted a letter. I read every single one of them, often with tissues nearby. I wish each one could have been in this collection. Thank you for being brave and telling your story. As Corey Ann Haydu said in her letter, "When it's something you own instead of something you fear, it's less shameful . . . Once that door opens, people walk through it. Once that door opens, everyone can breathe a little easier. Once that door opens, it's a little less lonely."

I'd like to have a huge group hug with the following people, all of whom helped to bring *Dear Heartbreak* to life:

Kate Farrell, my editor at Holt, who always says, "Yes! Yes, let's do *that*!" whenever I get an idea in my head, and who has one of the biggest hearts of anyone I know. Brenda Bowen, my endlessly passionate and kind agent, who helped to birth this project right alongside me with good cheer and the quiet calm of the very best sea-captains. Thank you to the agents of each author in the collection, who were down with them baring their souls. So much love to everyone at Macmillan who put their hearts into this book.

I'd also like to give a shout-out to Cheryl Strayed, whose *Dear Sugar* column inspired this project and many of its writers.

Finally, I'd like to thank the people who have loved *Dear Heartbreak*'s adult and teen writers well, patched us up, and given us reasons to believe that love is possible. But I most want to acknowledge (not necessarily *thank*) the people or situations that allowed us to gain the wisdom to love ourselves. Self-love became an unexpected theme in this book, and the wise words of these authors have shown me that there is much to be grateful for on this journey—even, crazily enough, some of the tough stuff.

Sending love to each and every one of you readers. And glitter. Because why not?

THE AUTHORS

Becky Albertalli is the author of *Simon vs. the Homo Sapiens Agenda*, now a major motion picture; *The Upside of Unrequited*; and the upcoming *Leah on the Offbeat* and *What If It's Us*. She used to write about unrequited love in her top-secret journals. Now she writes about unrequited love in books for teenagers. She lives with her family in Atlanta, and you can visit her online at beckyalbertalli.com.

Adi Alsaid is the author of several young adult books, including *Let's Get Lost* and *North of Happy*. He was born and raised in Mexico City, where he now lives and spills hot sauce on things.

Libba Bray is the #1 *New York Times* bestselling author of the Gemma Doyle trilogy (*A Great and Terrible Beauty, Rebel Angels, The Sweet Far Thing*); the Michael L. Printz Award–winning *Going Bovine*; *Beauty Queens*, a *Los Angeles Times* Book Prize finalist; and *The Diviners* series. She is also one-quarter of the all-YA-author rock band Tiger Beat. Originally from Texas, Libba lives in Brooklyn, New York, with her family and two sociopathic cats.

Mike Curato is an author and illustrator best known for his picture book series Little Elliot. He has illustrated several books for other authors, such as *What If . . .* by Samantha Berger, *All the Way to Havana* by Margarita Engle, and the well-loved pro-homo picture book *Worm Loves Worm* by J. J. Austrian. Mike is working on his first YA graphic novel, *Flamer*, about a fourteen-year-old boy who is coming to terms with his sexual identity while being bullied at a scout camp, with near-fatal consequences.

Heather Demetrios is the author of several young adult novels and countless love letters. When she isn't spending time in imaginary places, she's traipsing around the world with her husband and fellow writer, Zach Fehst. Heather is a recipient of the PEN New England Susan P. Bloom Discovery Award for her debut novel, *Something Real*. Her other novels include *Exquisite Captive*, *I'll Meet You There*, and *Bad Romance*. She has an MFA in Writing from Vermont College of Fine Arts. Find out more about Heather and her books at heatherdemetrios.com and come say hi on Twitter (@HDemetrios).

Amy Ewing is the author of the *New York Times* bestselling Lone City trilogy. She lives in New York City, navigating the minefield that is single city living and traveling as much as possible to soothe the heartbreaks along the way. You can find her at amyewingbooks.com, and on Twitter and Instagram (@amyewingbook).

Since he was a child, **Zach Fehst** has read everything he could get his hands on—even if it was only the back of a cereal box. Now, he mostly reads and writes speculative fiction filled with mystery and adventure. Before he started writing, he hosted the Emmy-nominated nature show *The Ultimate Guide to the Awesome* on the Discovery Kids Network. He's married to author Heather Demetrios. His first novel is forthcoming from Simon and Schuster. Find him on Twitter: @zachfehst.

Gayle Forman is an award-winning, internationally bestselling author. Her books include *I Have Lost My Way, Leave Me, Just One Day, Just One Year, I Was Here, Where She Went,* and *If I Stay,* which was made into a major motion picture. Gayle's work has been published in more than forty countries. She lives in Brooklyn, New York, with her family.

Corey Ann Haydu is the author of several critically acclaimed young adult and middle-grade novels, including *OCD Love Story, Rules For Stealing Stars,* and *The Careful Undressing of Love.* In 2013 she was chosen as a *Publishers Weekly* Flying Start. Her books have been Junior Library Guild Selections, Indie Next Selections, and BCCB Blue Ribbon Selections. She currently lives in Brooklyn with her husband, her daughter, her dog, and a wide selection of cheese in case of any heartbreaks or heartaches.

Varian Johnson is the author of several novels, including *The Great Greene Heist*, an ALA Notable Children's Book Selection, and his latest mystery, *The Parker Inheritance*. A die-hard romantic, Varian has dated three girls named Erika—but not at the same time—and they all broke his heart. Also, if Erika A. is reading this, he would like his sweater back.

A.S. King has been called "One of the best YA writers working today" by the *New York Times Book Review*. She is the author of highly acclaimed crossover novels, including her 2016 release *Still Life with Tornado*, 2015's surrealist *I Crawl Through It*, the 2012 Los Angeles Times Book Prize–winner *Ask the Passengers*, and 2011 Michael L. Printz Honor Book *Please Ignore Vera Dietz*, among others. After fifteen years living self-sufficiently and teaching literacy to adults in Ireland, she now lives in Pennsylvania with her weird family.

Nina LaCour is the award-winning and national bestselling author of five novels, most recently the 2018 Michael L. Printz Award–winning *We Are Okay*. She enjoys writing books about heartbreak as well as consuming art, films, and music on the subject. She lives in the San Francisco Bay Area with her wife and daughter, both of whom keep her heart firmly intact.

At sixteen, **Kim Liggett** left her rural midwestern town for New York City to pursue a career in music. Along with lending her voice to hundreds of studio recordings, she was a backup singer for some of the biggest rock bands in the '80s. Kim spends her free time studying the tarot and scouring Manhattan for vials of rare perfume and the perfect egg-white cocktail.

Kekla Magoon is the author of nine novels, including *The Rock and the River, How It Went Down, X: A Novel* (with Ilyasah Shabazz), and the Robyn Hoodlum Adventures series. She has received an NAACP Image Award, the John Steptoe New Talent Award, two Coretta Scott King Honors, the Walter Award Honor, the In the Margins Award, and been longlisted for the National Book Award. She also writes nonfiction on historical topics. Kekla conducts school and library visits nationwide and serves on the Writers' Council for the National Writing Project. Kekla holds a BA from Northwestern University and an MFA in Writing from Vermont College of Fine Arts, where she now serves on faculty. Visit her online at keklamagoon.com.

Sarah McCarry is the author of the novels *All Our Pretty Songs, Dirty Wings*, and *About A Girl*, the editor and publisher of the chapbook series Guillotine, the media coordinator for The Doula Project, and the executive director of the Eve Kosofsky Sedgwick Foundation. Her work has been shortlisted for the

Lambda Award, the Norton Award, and the Tiptree Award, and she has received fellowships from the MacDowell Colony, the Joint Quantum Institute, and the Launchpad Writers' Workshop.

Sandhya Menon is the *New York Times* bestselling author of *When Dimple Met Rishi* and *From Twinkle, With Love.* She lives in Colorado with her high school sweetheart, who holds the distinguished honor of never having broken her heart.

Cristina Moracho is the author of *Althea & Oliver* (Viking, 2014) and *A Good Idea* (Viking, 2017). She received an MFA in creative writing from Brooklyn College. A fan of true crime stories, coffee ice cream, and punk rock shows, she lives with her dog in Red Hook, Brooklyn, where she is teaching herself to play the guitar and read tarot cards while writing her next book.

Jasmine Warga lives and writes in Cincinnati, Ohio. She is the author of *My Heart and Other Black Holes* and *Here We Are Now.* Her books have been translated into more than twenty different languages and optioned for film. She made many mistakes in high school, one of which was dyeing her hair purple.

Ibi Zoboi holds an MFA in Writing for Children and Young Adults from Vermont College of Fine Arts. Her writing has been published in *The New York Times Book Review, The Horn*

Book Magazine, and *The Rumpus*, among others. Her debut novel, *American Street*, a National Book Award finalist, was published by Balzer + Bray, an imprint of HarperCollins Publishers. Her next YA novel, *Pride*, is due out in fall 2018. Her middle-grade debut, *My Life as an Ice-Cream Sandwich*, is forthcoming from Dutton/Penguin Books. Ibi has been married to the love of her life for sixteen years, and they share a home in Brooklyn with their three children. You can find her online at ibizoboi.net.